EXODUS TO BERLIN

EXODUS
TO BERLIN

The Return of the Jews to Germany

PETER LAUFER

IVAN R. DEE
Chicago 2003

Library of Congress Cataloging-in-Publication Data:
Laufer, Peter.
    Exodus to Berlin : the return of the Jews to Germany / Peter Laufer.
      p. cm.
    Includes bibliographical references and index.
    ISBN 1-56663-529-2 (alk. paper)
     1. Jews, Soviet—Germany—Berlin—History—20th century. 2. Jews—Europe, Eastern—Migrations. 3. Europe, Eastern—Emigration and immigration. 4. Berlin (Germany)—Emigration and immigration. 5. Antisemitism—Germany—Berlin. 6. Berlin (Germany)—Ethnic relations. I. Title.

DS135.G4B4654 2003
305.892'4043155'09049—dc21   200304224

With love to Sheila,

herzlichen Dank for my roots

Preface □ The Exodus of Jews to—
of All Places—Germany

JEWS AND GERMANS have suffered from a love-hate relationship—or at least a tolerate-hate relationship—since the Crusaders first rampaged across Europe. In one generation Jews are
protected by Germans; in another they are massacred.

Exodus to Berlin is the little-known story of the unexpected
resurgence of the Jewish community in Germany, which began
after the Berlin Wall fell, and the concurrent rise there of neo-
Nazi, racist, nationalistic, and anti-Semitic violence. As the
twenty-first century began, Germany found itself in the ironic
position of being home to the fastest-growing population of
Jews in the world. This unexpected surge of Jews into Germany
not only surprised both Jews and Germans, it occurred without
much of the world noticing. As I was finishing the research for
this book I encountered a friend, a grammar school teacher who
had taught one of my sons, and I told him of my work on this
project. He joined a parade of others shocked by the story
of Jews and neo-Nazis rising simultaneously in reunified Germany.

"Why would Jews want to live where the biggest slaughter of
Jews took place?" he fumed at me. "As a Jew I'm speaking," he
made clear. "And here come the right-wing scum again!"

Despite his commonplace concern, *Exodus to Berlin* is a
story of hope, renewal, and redemption.

TODAY IN GERMANY, the people with the guns are on the side of the Jews. Since the end of World War II, police protect Jews, their community, and their institutions. Until the fall of the Soviet Union and Eastern European communism, protecting Jews in postwar Germany was a relatively easy task. The Jewish community in Germany was tiny—virtually wiped out by the Nazis and shrinking fast as most survivors died or emigrated. All that changed sharply after the Berlin Wall fell.

Starting in 1989 a growing exodus of Jews from the former Soviet bloc has enriched Berlin and the rest of Germany with renewed elements of a vibrant Jewish subculture. The nation whose very name justifiably invoked fear and hatred in Jews around the world is surprised to be waking up to synagogues filled for services, bagels and blintzes in new restaurants sporting Hebrew-language signs, and the exotic strains of Klezmer music in clubs and street festivals. Tens of thousands of mostly Russian and Ukrainian Jews are seeking and receiving sanctuary in Germany from the anti-Semitism, violence, and economic chaos that distort the former Soviet Union and its former satellites. These Jews, many of them highly educated professionals, are often ignorant of the details of the faith of their ancestors. After all, practicing any religion other than communism had been for them an invitation to a nightmare of state-sponsored discrimination, brutality, and even murder in their former homelands. To this day, despite many genuine political reforms, Jews in the former Soviet Union are still at risk despite laws against national, racial, and religious persecution. Merely being Jews by birth still marks them for trouble in a land where some identity papers continue to label them as "Jew," not Russian, Ukrainian, or any other ethnically or geographically defined population group.

This modern exodus to Berlin and Germany has been encouraged and underwritten by the German government since 1990, soon after the fall of the Berlin Wall. By 2003 well over

100,000 Jews had made the journey from the former Soviet Union to Germany. There they find a wide range of generous, government-provided benefits to help them establish themselves in their new home. There has also been a warm welcome from many German Christians.

Nonetheless, the idea of Jews moving to Germany remains repugnant, or at least bizarre, for many—such as my disgusted schoolteacher friend.

Acknowledgments

WITHOUT THE TENACIOUS and creative reporting of journalist Jeff Kamen, this book would not exist. Together Jeff and I produced the documentary film *Exodus to Berlin*. We shared many of the interviews and experiences recounted in this book. Jeff's endless energy, his intuition for finding news in unexpected places, and his skill for persuading even the most hesitant to talk, all helped develop our sources and material. Jeff's pictures adorn this book: the cover image and the interior portraits are stills of his cinematography. During production of the film, and while working on other projects, I've learned much about myself and my profession from Jeff Kamen. I'm proud to call him friend and colleague. And I thank him for his gracious help.

Critical field support came from Berlin-based journalist Alisa Roth, who conducted some crucial interviews for the project. Other colleagues read early drafts. Terry Phillips, Tom Steinberg, Alex Roth, and Sheila Swan Laufer all helped mold the narrative. Terry Phillips managed the Russian translations. Michael Laufer and Gerda Dinwiddie worked with me translating the German.

Fellowships and foundation support for *Exodus to Berlin* from the John J. McCloy fellowships, the Robert Bosch Foundation, and the RIAS Berlin Commission were most helpful. Rainer Hasters, the executive director at RIAS and an early supporter of this work, deserves particular appreciation. George Papagiannis and the staff at Internews Network provided needed Washington, D.C., office space.

Assignments in Germany during my years as an NBC News correspondent, along with stringing duties in Germany for CBS and ABC radio, resulted in notes I was able to take advantage of for the book, as did articles I wrote for the Prague-based magazine *Pozor, Europe* magazine, and *Penthouse* (a special thanks to *Penthouse* editor Peter Bloch for his enthusiasm).

Several others influenced the project. Thanks to Sigrid Akkermann, Petra Schibrowski, and Claudio Funke in Berlin; Bill Sinrich in London; Mark Bauman in Washington; Wolfgang Linz in New York; and Markos Kounalakis, Mark Allen, and Chris Slattery in San Francisco. Kathy Talbert at D-J Word Processing in Santa Rosa, California, did a generous job transcribing tapes. Shona Weir provided logistical support.

I wish to acknowledge the fine work of Frank Stovicek, who designed and maintains the *Exodus to Berlin* website. Please visit it at www.exodustoberlin.com.

And finally, thanks to my father Thomas Laufer for coming to America and to my mother Eva Laufer for my optimism.

P. L.

Sonoma County, California
April 2003

Contents

EXODUS TO BERLIN

North
Sea

DENMARK

Baltic Sea

N

Greifswald
Hamburg

Bremen

NETHERLANDS

Hanover

Berlin
Potsdam
EAST
GERMANY
Guben
Peitz

POLAND

Cologne
Bonn

Leipzig

BELGIUM

LUX.

Frankfurt

WEST
GERMANY

CZECHOSLOVAKIA

FRANCE

Stuttgart

Munich

0   50   100 Miles
0   50 100 Kilometers

SWITZERLAND

AUSTRIA

**Germany
After WWII**

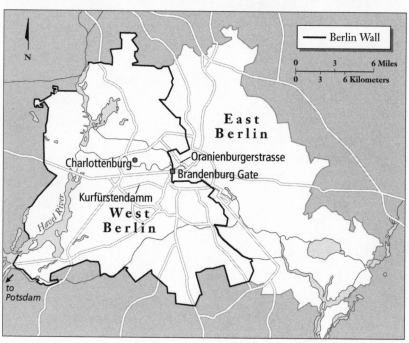

N

Berlin Wall

0   3   6 Miles
0   3   6 Kilometers

East
Berlin

Charlottenburg
Oranienburgerstrasse
Brandenburg Gate

Kurfürstendamm

West
Berlin

Havel River

to
Potsdam

1 □ *A Reluctant Move to Germany*

DR. ALEXANDRA BERMANT is a staff physician at a clinic on the outskirts of Berlin, in the state of Brandenburg, in what used to be East Germany. Sometimes her patients recognize her Russian accent and tell her she does not belong in Germany. But most of them are warm and grateful for her care. Like her teenage children, Olga and Vladimir, Dr. Bermant is delighted to have escaped the anti-Semitism and uncertainty that etch Russia today.

"I didn't want to leave Russia because I love Russia," she says from the comfort of her flat in the heart of the middle-class Russian immigrant community, the Charlottenburg neighborhood of Berlin. "I have my mother tongue there. I have all my friends there. It was very difficult for me to come here, especially to Germany." She winces as she bites out the word "Germany."

Under the surface of her current prosperity, Dr. Bermant is keenly aware of being resented, not only by prejudiced Germans but by Jews who escaped communism before the Berlin Wall fell. Back then, leaving the Soviet Empire was a serious challenge.

"The Jews from Russia who have been here maybe twenty years, they oppose us very strongly because they think we came too late, that we didn't have any difficulties, that we are this so-called butter immigration, that we came only to get something from the Germans." In fact, she says, her economic circumstances were quite comfortable in Russia.

She gets out the family photos. A group picture of her as a

medical student in a white coat with her peers and professors. A smiling little girl with a long braid and a dog. On a farm petting a cow with little Vlad. Bundled up against a Russian winter in a fur-trimmed sheepskin coat. At home with her children's father, a successful doctor who stayed in Russia. On a skiing vacation with the family. Another vacation with the New York City skyline in the background. On a camel in the desert. Underwater, diving off the Israeli coast. Life was not drab and austere in the Soviet Union for Alexandra Bermant.

Her prime motivation for leaving was fear that her son would be conscripted into the Russian military and sent to fight in its war in Chechnya. "I didn't want to go to Israel. I love Israel for a vacation, but I don't want to live there. We couldn't get to America. That was very difficult. We got official permission from the Germans to go to Germany. My mother told me, 'You must do it for your children. You must not be so selfish. You must not think only of yourself.' I was very happy in Russia at the time. I didn't want to leave."

Despite underlying concerns about German history and contemporary prejudice, she says, "We feel safe here in Berlin, as safe as in Russia, anyway. But in the small villages where I work in Brandenburg and where the people are not as progressive as in Berlin, I often see the skinheads who are against foreigners, against Jews, against every normal person. That's why sometimes I'm afraid. When I am alone at night and I'm driving through the countryside making my emergency house calls, sometimes I'm afraid because they can be very drunk. They notice my accent immediately, the first thing." She says she's encountered thugs who are so drunk they don't know their own names, "but they notice my accent and they're very hostile. They say, 'You are a foreigner.' And the next thing they say is, '*Ausländer raus!*' [Foreigners out!]. It's happened many times."

I join her for grand rounds at her hospital. The atmosphere is relaxed, cordial, and professional as she explains her cases to her fellow doctors. "I'm not the best," she says modestly, "but

I'm confident that I help my patients." She has clearly earned and enjoys the respect of her peers. She talks with them and her patients in fluent German, then switches to more than adequate English to chat with me. The old East German hospital is refurbished, the equipment relatively modern. As rounds end, she shares summary comments and smiles with the head doctor on duty. Their white coats against the white walls of the hospital accentuate their animated faces as they work together.

Alexandra Bermant

Life is good for Dr. Bermant in Berlin. She enjoys meandering along the Kurfürstendamm, the premier shopping boulevard on the western side of the city. "I'm feeling at home here. I like it. I like Ku'damm," she says, driving slowly past the elegant shops, French-sounding cabaret music on the car radio. "It's so dear. It's as if I were born here. It looks a little bit like Leningrad, no? And it's not as huge as London and New York. I know it pretty well now. These nice old buildings, many green parks. I'm feeling at home here. That's why I like it."

Her son Vladimir agrees: "I feel very comfortable in Berlin, first of all because I know people. I've got loads of friends here, both Jewish and non-Jewish. And I know places to go in Berlin. I know the nightlife. I feel very comfortable when I am out in Berlin, especially in the western part."

The night we were talking together Vladimir was going off to Blue, a *schickie-mickie* disco frequented by a fast crowd of Berliners. There a friend would be celebrating her birthday. Vlad smiles in anticipation of his pending evening. What's going to happen there, I ask. "Oh, what usually happens in discos and clubs and stuff, I suppose," he laughs, "people amusing themselves, or doing their best to amuse themselves." Vlad spent his childhood in the Soviet Union, he's attending a boarding school in Great Britain, he comes home to his mother's house in Berlin.

Where are you from? I ask him. Who are you?

"I suppose you can only say I'm Jewish, because I don't have a sense of belonging to a country. I don't really have a sense of homeplace because I just live where I live. It's not important for me at all. I could well imagine going to university in the States. I'm not sure where I'm going to work." His English is quite British and precise. "Place is not a problem for me."

Berlin in particular is not a problem for Vladimir. Despite its history, he too feels at home when he's in his mother's neighborhood.

"In western Berlin it's quite a common thing to see," he says about being Jewish in Charlottenburg, "because there are officially ten thousand Jews living in Berlin, and about twice as many Jews unofficially, when you count those who are half Jewish and all that stuff. In the eastern part of Berlin, where I used to live five or six years ago, it was different. I used to encounter racism at school. This has changed, I think, for the most part because Jews are now such a common thing in Berlin. We're just part of everyday life here."

This healthy, safe, self-assured young man agrees it can be construed as odd that he feels so comfortable in Berlin as an immigrant Jew, considering the city's relatively recent past. "I suppose if you consider the historical background of the Holocaust, it is strange. But western Berlin has been under the Allies' control for the last fifty years, meaning it's been a civilized Western city. And having Jews in a civilized Western city is not strange, is not odd at all. It's normal." He smiles and looks up at the ceiling, gathering a further thought. "If you look at the places where Jews live, most of the time it's Charlottenburg, Wilmersdorf, places like that. There are hardly any in the eastern part. I think it has to do with the last fifty years." And that helps explain the taunting he received as a schoolboy on the eastern side of the city, which had been in the Soviet sector of occupied Berlin.

But Vlad sees indications, even in western Berlin, of the past. "Sometimes you see skinheads, or sometimes you see bikers with swastikas on their jackets or anti-Semitic tattoos. But it happens everywhere in the world, I think. I've seen people like that in the UK." He says Berlin could be his future home, no problem. "Yes, of course, why not. It's a place that's just as good as London or any other place. I could well imagine having a job here."

It is a crisp and clear winter day, unusually balmy for Berlin at this time of year. Fallen leaves still litter the paving stones on the street in front of the apartment house. Dr. Bermant and her son walk to their car for a shopping trip. In an elegant Russian-language bookstore in Charlottenburg, she and Vlad browse the titles and chat with the shopkeepers in Russian. "I think Jewish people who come to Berlin should initially feel pretty safe," says Vlad. "When some people arrive," he's speaking slowly and thoughtfully, "they've got some misconceptions to do with German history, all the Nazi stuff. But I think in the western part of the city definitely it's now forgotten." He stops himself. "Or," he hesitates, "it's not forgotten, but people have turned away from that and turned toward moral standards which are more similar to normal ones, you see?"

Vladimir Bermant knows from firsthand experience how much better his life has been in Germany than it was back in mother Russia. "If I were writing a letter to someone who lives in Russia, or one of the other countries that once belonged to the Soviet Union, someone who still lives there and who wants to come to Germany to live here, I would probably tell him that it will be better here than it is there. I would tell him that he could feel safe, and he would be safe, and he would enjoy his life here after a period of getting used to the new environment, of learning the language, and making new friends. After one or two years he would feel perfectly fine."

For this postwar and post-Wall emigré, the problematic history of Germany and Jews is not an immediate concern, especially compared with the contemporary anti-Semitism Vlad remembers from his native land. "It's very odd in Russia, because most of the population sort of despise Jews and think Jews inferior to them. But, on the other hand, every time someone invents something, or someone just achieves something, they generally assume he must be Jewish because he's clever. Still they will hate him, and the general image is still of Jews as an inferior people."

Vlad hops out of the car on the Kurfürstendamm, in front of a Pizza Hut. A yellow double-decker bus—Route 119—passes by, the billboard stretched across its flank calling out *Wodka Gorbatschow*; it's an ad for Gorbachev brand vodka. The bus heads east, past the tower of the Kaiser Wilhelm Memorial Church, the jagged steel cupola that secures its war-damaged roof glittering in the winter sunshine. The wide sidewalks are jammed with couples arm-in-arm, businessmen on the march, families strolling and window-shopping. Rolex watches tick next to strands of pearls. Full-length furs fill show windows. Another double-decker cruises by, this one advertising furniture and shouting out the store's slogan, written in English: "Who's Perfect?" Around a corner and up a quiet side street is one of the Holocaust memorials spotted around the city. It's a plain brick wall. Affixed to it is a Star of David, the dates 1933–1945, and the names of places where Jews were slaughtered during the war—the Warsaw Ghetto, the Sachsenhausen concentration camp just outside Berlin in Brandenburg, and seventeen other death camps. Heaps of fresh flowers overflow on the sidewalk in front of the wall. An old Berlin cop keeps watch, smiling at tourists and carrying a machine gun.

Back at the family's elegant Charlottenburg apartment, Vladimir's mother brings out her Soviet-era documents. "This is the birth certificate, that's mine and that's for my son," she says pointing out the details on official papers with Cyrillic lettering.

8

"It doesn't say that I am Jewish, but it tells you that my papa is a Jew and my mother is a Jew. Here," she says about Vlad's papers. "That's the father, his name," and she points to the line below the name, "and that he is Jewish." And another name, "The mother, and that she is also Jewish." Their Soviet-era passports also mark them as Jews. "First the surname, then your name, then your father's name, the date of birth, and the fifth paragraph is the nationality. That's why it was a common joke in Russia that Jews were invalids according to Paragraph Five." The point being that because Jews' passports identify them as Jews, they are handicapped. "It was unpleasant because you didn't have an equal chance to get a job, to get to the university." She tells stories of being ostracized by some professors during her university days, told that because she was a Jew they did not want her as a student. It was prejudice, she says, that slowed her progress through medical school.

She serves coffee and cookies. The apartment is furnished modern, but the coffee cups are decorated with painted flowers, the handles brushed with gold, and the silver is equally ornate. "It is amazing," Dr. Bermant agrees, that the Jewish community is thriving in Berlin, "but I'm not sure it has a future because so many people oppose foreigners." And she questions the solidarity of the Jewish population in Germany. "I'm not sure it really is a community," she says about the Jews in Berlin, "because they are not so united, the people. They are so different."

Alexandra Bermant did not grow up in a household where the Jewish religion was actively observed. "I didn't know about being Jewish until I was maybe seven. My family is Jewish, but they are not traditional. That's why the prejudice I encountered was difficult for me. I'm not feeling myself very Jewish, I'm feeling myself more Russian."

Until a day in the second grade.

"Some girl in class told me I was a dirty Jew. I can remember it very well. I asked my grandma about it. I knew I wasn't dirty, but I didn't know what 'Jew' was." She laughs at the absurdity.

"She told me about dirty Jews and the whole story about them." She sighs as she explains away her long-ago classmate. "The girl came from a very simple family, and it was a common word if you wanted to insult someone. I'm sure she didn't mean it. She wasn't anti-Semitic. She had just heard it many times from her parents. She was not a nasty girl. She was just someone who said that."

Settled as she is in Berlin, Dr. Bermant seems tied to Russia. "I don't lose contact with Russian culture." She reads Russian literature, she attends Russian theatre and concerts. "I love Russian music. I'm very touched. I can cry when I hear Tchaikovsky or Rachmaninoff." She is not an assimilated immigrant, and as she thinks aloud about her identity, conflicts loom. "I don't want to be German. I don't want to merge with the Germans completely, I want to stay with Russian culture. The Germans feel themselves very superior to the foreigners. I hate it." Her eyes narrow, she shakes her head. "I don't think the Germans are so superior. They are just normal people. There are bad people and there are very nice people. The same with the Jews, or the Russians, or any other. I think my home is in Berlin, but I am not completely German." She approaches these questions pragmatically. "We applied for the German citizenship because it's more convenient. It makes traveling much simpler."

2 □ *German Schoolgirls Talk About Skinheads*

AN ENCOUNTER with a couple of teenage girls—contemporaries of Vladimir Bermant—shopping on the Ku'damm, in Berlin from the provinces of surrounding Brandenburg, reinforces Vlad's optimism about his peers. Seventeen-year-old Nicolette Corduan was an exchange student in Texas and came back with smooth American English, punctuated with mall slang. A subtle nose ring and a row of silver earrings, blue eyeshadow contrasting with her black mascara and deep red lipstick, all help her appear older than high school age.

"Our town, where we go to school," she says when asked about skinheads at her school, "it's like, there are a couple of people running around with—like—those special jackets and shoes and stuff, always talkin' about 'We don't like foreign people' and stuff. I think it's not really a serious problem. I mean, it's bad. But those people are just following peer-group pressure. When they get older they just grow out of it and realize it's not really smart what they're doing."

Stephanie Will, minus the heavy makeup and jewelry and looking more like a schoolgirl than her friend, says she doesn't really know those students who dress up and act like skinheads. "In the town where I live there are quite a few skinheads," she says, sighing. "There are some violent acts too. They act pretty violent against, like, older people and sometimes against, like, foreign people. I think most of them are just following the group and they want to be cool." Her school time in South Dakota is evident from the "yup" and "yeah" and "like" that she sprinkles throughout her crisp English as she tries to express some understanding of what motivates the deviates. "Young people don't have so many chances to do something in their free time without paying a lot of money, so they're trying to find something they can do. I think they're just following."

Nicolette says she's convinced the attacks are random. "They don't look for Jews. Sometimes they beat up people, but it's not even foreign people. Sometimes it's just people like us who wear baggy pants. And Jews? No. Because they don't really know who the Jews are. They just look for the color of the skin or what people look like." After thinking about these hoodlums and their actions, she hesitates to call them neo-Nazis. "It's kind of hard to call them skinheads at all. Where we live, it's just peer-group pressure, I'd call it. Where we live there are not a lot of foreign people. Here in Berlin there are so many foreign people, you hear so many languages when you just sit in the subway or walk around. People here have contact with foreign people and know the different cultures. Where we live, we don't have that many foreign people. So the people who want to be skinheads, they're intolerant and prejudiced." She shakes her head and her eyes look around as she searches for an explanation for their actions. "They don't even know foreign people, so that's like the worst thing. The contact with foreign people is missing, and therefore they're prejudiced."

"Most skinheads are just wannabes," says Stephanie. "Most of them just want to be right in the middle of the action. They want to be somewhere. They want to be right in the spotlight, and they want to do something to be there. They want to have power. They're trying to be something so that they're in the news."

Public education policies add to the problem, Nicolette points out, describing the history curricula in Brandenburg. "In history class we get to know about the Nazi period in tenth

12

grade. And we don't get all through it. The problem is, people can leave school in the tenth grade and not hear even once about that period, the Second World War and the Holocaust. They never hear about it." Nonetheless, she says, her town's school board just cut back the hours required for tenth-grade history study. "Teachers can't even get through it all. The problem is, many young people where we live have never heard about the Holocaust and all that. They have no education about it. That's why prejudices come up."

The two of them continue their promenade down the Ku'-damm.

I wander off into the Berlin dusk. The city throbs. Berliners feel an affinity for New York. They like to think the two cities share the same kind of pulsating energy. There's truth to that comparison. Berlin is another city that never sleeps. The interior lights of the S-Bahn trains create a continuing and unpredictable show of motion, threading over streets and sidewalks, between buildings. The whine of their electric motors speeding up and slowing down, the scrape of steel wheels on track, combine with the shifting engine noises of street traffic, bicycle bells, and the clatter of footfalls to make a twenty-four-hour symphony. The mix of trash-filled vacant lots and construction sites, the bland postwar replacement buildings punctuated by restored old landmarks and ultramodern skyscrapers all create an unending and ever-changing stage set. The sewer stink in the humid summers or the sweet gag of brown coal smoke in the winter months offsets the too common urban perfume of spilled beer and urine. Flower stalls offer color on most commercial corners, as do newsstands with their loud collection of papers and magazines. *Wurst* vendors provide needed beer with their seemingly endless choice of sausages.

My favorite *wurst* seller works Alexanderplatz at the entrance to the S-Bahn station. He wears a contraption that is like a combination of a backpack and a cigarette girl's tray. The tray is a gas grill. He cooks the *wurst* as he parades back and forth on the sidewalk. Strapped to his back is a gas bottle to fuel the grill. Attached to the harness is a pole to hold a rainbow-colored umbrella over him for protection against Berlin's frequent drizzle.

At the Kaufhof department store on Alexanderplatz, a worker is laboring at the show windows with an electric grinder, trying to polish off offensive graffiti scratched into the glass. "I think they do this only for fun," he tells me with disgust. "Young people—they haven't work. They sit around here," he gestures to the wide-open space of Alexanderplatz, "and they have nothing to do for fun. And they scratch the windows, I don't know why. It's a crazy thing, I think. It's not okay. It's work for me. But it's not okay."

Around the corner a butcher arranges sausage after sausage in a refrigerator case. I easily lose track of the varieties of potatoes, bread, and sausage for sale in Berlin. A jackhammer breaks up asphalt: Alexanderplatz is another of Berlin's endless construction sites. A vegetable and fruit stand run by Middle Eastern immigrants adds more color to this street scene. Their produce fills boxes on tables set up in front of a graffiti-covered construction barrier. One of the vendors is trimming onion greens. "Where are you from," he asks me. I tell him California. "*Ja*, America," he says with a smile. I ask him the same question. "From Palestine," he says in German, complaining about the Israelis he fled from in 1948.

Commuters transfer from streetcars and parade across the Alex, disappearing down into the U-Bahn station. It's a silent march, no talking, just footsteps and the low hum of the trains filtering up the stairs.

3 □ Germans and Immigrant Jews Struggle to Coexist

AT GERMANY'S all-news television channel, NTV, News Director Markus Föderl commissioned a series of spots designed to promote an understanding of the fact that Germany is a nation of immigrants. Called "Together Instead of Apart," the campaign draws attention to the multicultural environment at NTV itself. One shows two newsroom employees smiling. They clearly are friendly colleagues; one is black and the other white.

"I'm normal," says one.

"I'm a normal German," says the other.

"I'm a normal South African German," is the response.

Then they say in duet, "But what's normal?" And they giggle, "Who knows?"

"The big issue is tolerance," Föderl tells me about the campaign when we meet at NTV. He looks like a TV anchor anywhere, especially where we're talking in the studio, against the stark blue background of the news set, the same flattering blue background that was used for official portraits to offset the harsh features of the longtime East German leader Erich Honecker.

Markus Föderl's words are far from any attempt at removed objectivity. He wants to use the power of his station to change the mentality of his community. "It's easy just to focus on right-wing attacks, but it's not only right-wing attacks. It's a matter of thinking and how you deal with your colleagues. It's easy to say,

'I'm against right-wing attacks.' But you have to show tolerance in everyday life. We try to show this with our campaign."

When they shot the spots, the crews at NTV were surprised to learn just how diverse their workforce is. "We discovered how many different people, with many different religions, opinions, sexual orientations, work with NTV." As the staff learned more about each other, Föderl says, they grew closer. "It had a very good effect making it clear that different people can work together perfectly if they are tolerant."

Marcus Föderl

Föderl is convinced of an ongoing need in Germany to educate the populace against prejudice. "I think it's not only a job for the media, it's a job for all of us. It's a question of tolerance and openness to different nations, to different orientations concerning, for instance, sex. It's a problem for the whole society, and we all have to deal with it."

MANY OFFICIAL and nongovernmental institutions fight prejudice in Germany. Because of its Nazi past and the xenophobia that shames unified Germany today, it is a country almost obsessed with combating bigotry. It's not easy. One Berlin social service agency provides teaching aids to help explain that there is no difference between German blood and the blood of foreigners. One set of these show-and-tell props consists of two actual blood bags, the type used to provide blood for transfusions. Both are filled with an identical red liquid. One is labeled "German blood." The other is labeled "other blood."

The Berlin government produces an ongoing series of television spots designed to teach tolerance. One shows a cartoon father and son in their living room. The son is lecturing the father. "A black man is born black," he explains. "He stays black when he is in the sun—and he dies black. But a white man is born pink and turns red in the sun. He turns blue when ill and grey when he dies." The father looks irritated and explodes, "That's all rubbish!" The son looks amused and says, "Dad, what's wrong? You've turned green!"

In another of the government spots, an actor dresses up in stereotypical costumes of four European nationalities while an announcer explains their differences. "Look, this is Pierre. He is a Frenchman. All Frenchmen are called Pierre." The backdrop shows the Seine and Notre Dame. "On his head," says the announcer, "he wears a beret. All Frenchmen wear berets. Under his arm he carries a baguette. French people live mainly on baguettes. Pierre can also speak." The announcer commands the Pierre character to say something. He responds with, "Ooo-la-la, ooo-la-la, ooo-la-la," and the announcer deadpans, "French people always say, 'Ooo-la-la.' Now you know what French people are like." Italians are described next, with pizza and a pistol replacing the beret and baguette. The actor, playing Marcello, says, "Tutti-frutti." As a Spaniard, the actor is Pepe; he eats paella, holds the red cape of a *torero*, and says, "Olé!" Finally the actor depicts a Berliner named Bolle. The announcer explains, "All Berliners are called Bolle. In one hand he holds a steering wheel. He needs it because he is a taxi driver. All Berliners are taxi drivers. In the other hand he has a tin of Berlin air.* All Berliners live mainly on Berlin air. Bolle can also speak," says the announcer, and Bolle replies, "Ich bin Berliner." The announcer adds, "Bolle says things like that because he is so quick-witted. All Berliners are quick-witted." In the final scene all four characters show off their costumes and props, and the an-

---

*Many Berliners like to ascribe what they consider the unique Berlin atmosphere to what they call the special Berlin *Luft*, its air.

nouncer intones, "So now you know what a Frenchman, an Italian, a Spaniard, and a Berliner is, and how to tell the difference."

Barbara John heads the Berlin government office in charge of foreigner affairs, the government department that authorizes the TV spots. She says the exodus of Jews to Berlin is a success, in part because of the extraordinary social help they receive from the government. "They are treated like recognized asylum seekers. So they are entitled to free housing. They get maintenance welfare money and they are entitled to free medical care. This can go on as long as they don't find a job. So for elderly people it continues for a very long time. They are entitled to a language course." Many are also candidates for education programs. "If they are not older than twenty-seven years they can qualify for training for a better job."

The portfolio for Barbara John's office is not just the needs of incoming Jews but all foreigners. She is well respected for her concern for immigrants' rights and for her relentless work to ease the integration of immigrants into Berlin's growing multicultural society. As we talk, she exudes a tired warmth. She clearly cares for her clients, but she acts somewhat weary about the endless work she faces, both as an advocate for the newcomers and a tutor for those cloister-minded fellow Germans she tries to counsel. A poster ubiquitous on Berlin billboards is another product of her office. Showing a couple of dozen friendly, smiling, and ethnically diverse faces, its headline shouts: "*Wir sind Berlin.*" We are Berlin. And in case the point is missed by some, the subheadline adds, "We are light and dark."

Because Berlin is again the German capital city, because it is a cosmopolitan center, because it has a history of both vibrancy and tolerance, and because of its large and growing Jewish community, most of the Jewish immigrants to Germany who must rely on government assistance ask to be resettled in Berlin. The city tries to be accommodating, says John. "Not everyone who wants to live in Berlin can come here. Berlin has taken a big

18

quota. It has taken more people than it should take because most of the Russian Jews want to live in a big city and Berlin is for them this big city." But plenty of Jews don't get the opportunity to settle in Berlin and end up being placed in remote villages where there are only a few other Jews in the neighborhood and no rabbi. Of course, those who need no state support can settle wherever they wish as soon as they receive legal status as immigrants.

There is no question that incoming Jews get preferential treatment over other immigrants to Germany. As soon as Jews apply to settle in Germany, they are awarded the status of "recognized asylum seekers." This means they do not need to wait for their cases to be adjudicated, as is the requirement for any other asylum seekers. While other refugees from chaos around the world wait for a hearing and a resolution of their cases, a wait that may last for months and even years, Jews immediately begin their new lives. Other refugees, while their status is pending, cannot resettle from refugee centers and are refused work permits. Even when they qualify as refugees they must serve a three-year waiting period before they are eligible to receive social entitlements such as those Jews enjoy immediately on arrival. Even then the terms are different. Other refugees don't receive as much of a cash stipend as do the Jews, and few are authorized to settle in Berlin. They're scattered across the country. Of course, some of those who apply for it are not granted refugee status and are sent back to their countries of origin. Others receive only temporary refugee status, pending changes back home. Plenty of refugees from the wars in the Balkans, for example, found their lives in Germany forcibly disrupted when the worst of the shooting stopped and they were sent back.

This double standard has the potential to generate resentment against the incoming Jews among others who seek asylum in Germany, but Barbara John insists that because of the Nazi past it's not a consequential problem. "Nobody really envies the Jewish immigrants for the little advantages they have now." Because so many of the Jews choosing to move to Germany are highly educated and well-trained professionals, she says, Germany's new Jews are thriving.

"*Wilkommen*," Barbara John says when I ask her what her message is for other Jews considering such a move. "They should come to Berlin, but they can do this only if they can make their own living. We want them to be here because we want creative people." She stumbles over her words and looks away as a stereotype tumbles out of her mouth. "We know that the Jewish immigrants are mostly either artists . . ." Another stumble. Perhaps she realizes that what she's saying—though it's positive praise—may sound like a form of prejudice. "They are very well qualified." Again the Jews are separated as different, even potentially threatening. "We know that their children are very ambitious. They are the best students in our schools." But she recovers. "So we would like them to be here, but at first they have to see that they get a job, and then there is no barrier for them to come to Berlin."

Will they find a welcome, or will they find resentment? I ask her.

A smile crosses her face. "No, they will find a warm welcome." Her voice is warm against the winter air. Her eyes, inviting. Her words express emotions backed by years of hard work to help create that welcome.

BORIS ROSENTHAL plays Klezmer music with his partner Igor Ginsburg in Berlin's Jewish clubs and restaurants, such as the popular eatery Rimon. *Israelische Spezialitäten* says the sign out front. Featuring fine Israeli wines and heaping plateloads of delicious Middle Eastern cuisine, Rimon is packed with diners looking for something different from a stereotypical German night out. They're enjoying not just the food but the Jewish-themed decor: Stars of David accent the walls. Waitresses slide past Rosenthal trying not to disturb his guitar picking or disrupt Ginsburg's attention as he closes his eyes and wails on his clarinet the mournful strains of this Eastern European Jewish folk music. Flower girls come in from Oranienburgerstrasse and work the tables.

During a break in the evening's music I ask Rosenthal why he moved from the former Soviet Union to Berlin.

"It's a difficult question," he says. "Actually, it was by chance. I didn't plan to come to Berlin. But now I feel as if I am a Berliner. And Berliners are not sour when I call myself a Berliner." He smiles. "I love this city. Like many cities in the world I've seen, it's a world capital. Maybe after New York City it's the number one city in the world. It's interesting for the culture, the politics, and for me as a musician and a teacher."

Rosenthal dismisses the Berlin past and tells me the city is entirely different from what it was in the thirties and forties, that for him—as a Jew and an immigrant—it is ideal. "Berlin is an international city. In Berlin, as in New York, there are many corners where many different nationalities from many different places of the world live. Turks, Americans, Russians, Jews. I can't call Berlin a German city today. I have seen many German cities, and Berlin is something different."

Who are you? I ask Rosenthal as he smiles under his bushy moustache and talks about his adopted city. He is anxious to get back to the dinner crowd and his music, but he spends a few more minutes talking about the unexpected political changes that led him to make Berlin his new home. Are you Ukrainian? I ask. Are you Jewish? Are you a Berliner? Are you on the road with a guitar and a packed suitcase, stopping off in Berlin?

"Okay," he interrupts my questions, "I am Jewish," he tells me in English, and then switches to German, *"und das ist gross geschrieben,"* to emphasize its importance—literally telling me that his Jewishness is written big. "I am Jewish. I was a Ukrainian, a socialist. I am that no more. I am Jewish. I like my religion. I can go to synagogue here in Berlin. This is possible. Obviously this is a German city"—he's not contradicting himself, he's talking about a political reality versus the cultural identifi-

cation he gave Berlin when he called it an international city—
"obviously the German politics and mentality are here. But that
does not interest me today. Because for me as a Jew, I can live as
a Jew here. I can play my Jewish music here. That was not possible for me for years in the Ukraine." In Germany, he says, his
music is judged by audiences for its quality, not its religion.
"When it's good, everyone is enthusiastic. When it's bad, that's
bad." He laughs. "I live here with all my spirit. I live here with
my heart. I live here as a Berliner."

He leans back in his chair content, smiling. I almost wish I
had not disturbed the moment by asking one more question. Do
you have no angst regarding the history here, that there could
again be problems for Jews? Boris Rosenthal nods. "Could be,"
he says. "I hope not, but it could be. I hope that kind of history
will never again happen." He puts his skull cap back on his balding head and joins his partner Igor Ginsburg in the dining room
for more Klezmer.

Boris Rosenthal's son Leonid is studying in Berlin. When I
meet with him a few evenings later, he tells me that he leads a
happy life as a Ukrainian Jew in Germany. "I go to the university. I have many friends. I believe that Berlin is a very nice city,
though there are many conflicts here, of course." He's a gregari-
ous fellow; his English is all but flawless. We talk in the open
space that still exists along so much of the path of the Wall. His
father is playing Klezmer music with Ginsburg and some others
on a makeshift stage near us; it's the site of the still-controversial
Berlin memorial to European Jews murdered during the Holocaust. In the mid-nineties a public call for entries solicited design ideas for the memorial. Drawings and models of the ideas
were displayed for public comment. The oddest one of the
bunch that sticks in my memory of the exhibition: railroad
tracks laid out to create the image of a menorah. The idea,
explained the amateur sculptor, was to remind the viewer of
both the trains used for deportation and a miracle of the Jewish
religion.

Leonid Rosenthal is bundled up against the cold in a pea coat with a baseball cap tight over his close-cropped hair. "To live here as a Jew, or to live here as an immigrant, you sometimes have problems." But he is worldly in his criticism. "I think in another place I would have the same problems."

He looks thoughtful, his eyes wide, and he chooses his words carefully when I ask him what types of problems he faces. "I think I will always feel I am a stranger here because I'm not German, and I think my German will never be that perfect. The people will always hear and know I am not German. I think it is also my way of life, which is different from the German way of life. Because of this I'm not—how do you say it?—I'm not totally integrated into the society."

The Jewish holidays and other religious observances create this difference, says Leonid. "Most of my friends who are Germans know that on Friday I can't go out with them at six o'clock because I am in synagogue." He smiles. "I don't think that it's bad that I'm different. Ten years ago I lived in Russia, and I was also different from the others. If I move to another country, to France or to America, or even," he shrugs, "Israel, I think I will be different from the others." Another smile as he explains why he thinks he will always be different. "When I go to America, I will be an immigrant. When I go to Israel, I'm not an Israeli. So I don't see anyplace in the world where I will be the same as the others." And that includes going back to the former Soviet Union. "In Russia I will have the same problems, as a Jew. Not as an immigrant but as a Jew." It's been ten years since Leonid last was in Russia. "I don't know the political situation there very well, but I'm very sure it will be the same."

So where is your home? I ask him. Again, his warm and engaging smile as he answers, "I have no idea." He shakes his head and says again, "I have no idea. I mean there are places that are very nice for me. For example, when I go to Israel I have many relatives there and I can speak openly without even thinking about racists or Nazis or anti-Semitism. I can go with *kippah* or

Mogen David, very proud," he says about his skull cap and Star of David jewelry. Leonid lets out a slight laugh. "Maybe Israel is the place where I can say I am nearest to my home. But not totally."

Why not try to make Germany a home, since he is living in Germany? "Because I'm an immigrant." Then another thought. "I don't want Germany to be my home. I can't speak with my relatives in Israel and tell them Germany is my home. I don't think I could ever say it." So why live in Germany? "Why live here? Because today I do like this place. I have many friends. My parents came here to Germany. I think they like it. I like it now. I don't know how it will be in two or three years. Maybe I will move to another country. But today, now, I like it very much here. There is always change. Potsdamerplatz," he states as an example, pointing out the scarred land where we're standing, the construction site in the middle of the city, "when you go away from Berlin and you come one month later, there will be so many things that will have changed. There are so many tourists. It is the capital of Germany. People from all over the world are here. You walk down the street and you meet tourists. I go to the university—there are so many people from other countries and it is very interesting to talk to them. I like it very much, yes."

Anti-Semitism motivated the family to leave their home, he says. "Of course it also exists here in Germany, but not official as in Russia. Germany is a democratic country, and Ukraine—I'm not sure whether it is democratic."

While Leonid Rosenthal expresses his delight with Berlin, "There are many places I wouldn't go. There are many districts in the eastern part, like Marzan or Hellersdorf, that I wouldn't go to." Not that staying away from these pockets where unemployed thugs occupy the street corners bothers him. "I have no reason to go there. When you open the newspaper you always read that they beat an African person or another. There are many Nazis. Because of this I wouldn't go there."

WEEKENDS IN BERLIN there is a vibrant flea market along Strasse-des-17-Juni near the Tiergarten S-Bahn station, called the Trödel und Kunstmarkt, the junk and art market. Filled with old German stuff—furniture, musical instruments, tools, books, memorabilia—it's a festive place to stroll. Stands offer *wurst* with beer and Turkish falafel prepared by Vietnamese proprietors. Usually street musicians hang out on the nearby Charlottenburger Bridge, playing for tips.

On a sunny winter day I stop and look at a stall filled with beautifully restored antique typewriters. An intense young man is busy cleaning one of them with a rag, polishing it. "It's an old one, from 1880," he tells me. It's a beautiful typewriter, we agree, and he tells me he's fixing it up for the transport and technology museum in Berlin. We talk some more, and I learn he's twenty-two years old, born and raised in Berlin, though he calls himself a Palestinian Muslim.

What do you think about the influx of Jews from the former Soviet Union, I ask. Is it good for Berlin? He stops polishing and answers directly. "Not all these people are good for Berlin, but most of them, yes." He returns to his polishing.

4 ☐ The Legacy of German Anti-Semitism

SIX HUNDRED YEARS before Bismarck united the German states into a single nation, Jews had been living and thriving in Berlin. The year 1244 is the earliest Jewish gravestone date found in the environs, in Spandau on the far west side of the city. Jews came north to get out of the path of the marauding Crusaders. Berlin then was two encampments, Berlin and Cölln, frontier trade ports and fishing villages straddling the river Spree. Early evidence of Jews in Berlin includes an order in 1295 from the weavers guild prohibiting members from buying yarn from Jewish merchants. At the time, Christians were forbidden from lending money in return for interest. Jews took advantage of this market niche and offered Berlin and Cölln merchants the opportunity to finance their growing trade ventures.

The Jewish community soon expanded to other businesses, competing with and therefore creating tension with other settlers. Butchers, for example, felt threatened when Jews marketed animal organs they did not choose to eat themselves. The city government acted in 1343, taxing Jews who butchered their own stock.

When in 1348 the bubonic plague arrived on the banks of the Spree, along with epidemics of influenza, smallpox, and typhus, disease quickly killed off a tenth of Berlin's population. Enough traumatized Berliners decided to blame a convenient "other," the Jews, for the deaths and sickness that Jews were no longer safe on the streets. Some Jews were falsely charged with poisoning the city's water supply and executed. Others were physically attacked both in public and in their own homes. In response, some Berlin Jews created their own enclosed ghetto, barricading an alley where many moved during the crisis. Elsewhere in Germany, Jews were forced into ghettos, their movement around cities and the countryside restricted. Jews were blamed for the plague that swept across Europe. Pogroms destroyed more than five hundred Jewish communities on the Continent; estimates of the toll in Germany include twelve thousand killed in Bavaria alone. "It would be hard to find," concluded the popular historian Will Durant, "before our time, or in all the records of savagery, any deeds more barbarous than the collective murder of Jews in the Black Death."

It was six years before the rights of Jews to live in Berlin were officially reestablished, July 6, 1354.

These were lawless and confusing times for all Berlin residents. Plenty of Christian Berliners joined their Jewish neighbors as victims of violent and barbaric punishments at the hands of mobs and governments.

In the early 1500s Jews were again banned from Berlin. German and other European Jews were under continuing assault, facing confiscation of property, banishment from their communities, and murder. In an early case of the "Blood Libel," Berlin Jews were charged with desecrating the Host and accused of having killed Christian children to obtain blood for rituals. Flight or forced baptism were often the only choices open to them to avoid persecution. Two particular cases were used as excuses for the Berlin expulsion. In 1500 seven Jews were arrested, and many others implicated, for the murder of a boy. Ultimately about thirty Jews were burned at the stake for the crime, which was called a ritual murder. In 1510 scores more Jews were arrested and dozens executed for stealing a monstrance holding two Hosts from a church. Those convicted of the boy's murder were ultimately exonerated by the courts, and the Elector of Brandenburg allowed Jews back into the city. But their stay was brief. The Elector's death triggered anti-Semitic riots; rioters blamed the Jews for poisoning him. An order in 1572 or 1573 expelling Jews demanded that they stay out of Berlin "for all eternity."

That fit fine with the aging Martin Luther's specific hopes for Jews. In *The Jews and Their Lies* he beseeched his readers "that you refuse to let them own houses among us. For they practice the same thing in their houses as they do in their schools. Instead, you might place them under a roof, or stable, like the Gypsies, to let them know that they are not lords in our country as they boast, but in exile as captives." He suggested "that you take away from them all of their prayer books and Talmuds wherein such lying, cursing, and blaspheming is taught." He called for "protection for Jews on highways [to] be revoked. For they have no right to be in the land . . . they should stay at home." Luther roils on in the pamphlet, with both more specific recommendations and plenty of rambling general condemnation. "Be on your guard against the Jews and know that where they have their schools there is nothing but the Devil's nest in which self-praise, vanity, lies, blasphemy, disgracing God and man, are practiced in the bitterest and most poisonous way as the Devils do themselves." Finally he writes, "In my opinion it will have come to this: if we are to stay clean of the Jew's blaspheming and not become partakers of it, we must separate, and they must leave our country."

It wasn't until 1650 that a select group of Jews was invited back to Berlin to conduct business, a number expanded on May 21, 1671, to fifty families of Jews, according to an official proclamation titled, "Admission of Fifty Families of Protected Jews." These fifty families, proclaimed the edict, would be allowed to "keep open stalls and booths, to sell cloth and similar wares, to deal in new and old clothes, and further, to slaughter in their houses and to sell what is above their needs or forbidden to them by their religion, and finally to seek their subsistence in any place where they live." This policy change opened the city gates to an initial immigration of a new Jewish community and the beginnings of the development of a German and Jewish cultural mélange. The community of the original fifty families was soon augmented by illegal immigration.

By 1743 those fifty families had grown to 333, for a total Jewish population in Berlin registered at 1,945. This was the year Moses Mendelssohn arrived at the gates of the city. As the philosopher's reputation grew, he worked to convince Jews that being German was not inconsistent with their religion, and to make clear to Christian Germans that Jews could be as German as they were. In 1750 Frederick the Great expanded the rights of Jews to allow for Jewish schools, synagogues, and cemeteries in Berlin, and the Jewish population increased to about 2 percent of the Berlin population. But their lives were not without government-imposed restrictions, from special taxes to prohibitions against practicing law and medicine, to a denial of participation in some of the upper reaches of society. One example occurred in 1763 when Frederick denied the nomination by his peers of Mendelssohn to the Prussian Academy of Sciences. The president of the Academy explained the veto by suggesting that Mendelssohn was missing only one requirement for royal approval, "a foreskin."

Berlin's flourishing Jewish community mobilized 450 troops for the 1812 liberation fight against French occupation and Napoleon as he and his defeated army retreated from Russia. That same year the Prussians finally granted citizenship rights to Jews, rights withdrawn just a few years later once Napoleon was no longer a threat to the city. The status of Jews in Germany differed during this period, depending on local laws in the dozens of independent states and various autonomous cities that made up the country. Nowhere were they accorded equal status with the Christian majority. Finally, in 1871, the constitution of Bismarck's united Germany mandated full citizenship rights to Jews.

As Berlin grew and prospered through the nineteenth century, so did the Jewish community, a community the city depended on for its rapid and successful economic development. In 1860 the Jewish population of Berlin was measured at 18,900. Just twenty years later that number had increased to 53,900. Many of the newcomers were *Ostjuden*, Jews from Eastern Europe. The bulk of these immigrants then—as is the case in Germany today—were refugees, exchanging prejudice and persecution in their hometowns for the relatively relaxed atmosphere of usually tolerant Berlin. Tolerant, but not without prejudice. Jews were banned from military and diplomatic service.

The Berlin stock market crashed in 1873. Looking to cast blame, some Berliners found the Jews among them easy targets, since so many had become successful entrepreneurs. The journalist Otto Glagau was one of those leading the charge, in the magazine *Gartenlaube*. A sample of his vitriol: "No longer should false tolerance and sentimentality, cursed weakness and fear, prevent us Christians from moving against the excesses, excrescences, and presumption of Jewry. No longer can we suffer to see the Jews push themselves everywhere to the front and to the top, to see them everywhere seize leadership and dominate public opinion. They are always pushing us Christians aside, they put us up against the wall, they take our air and our breath away. The richest people in Berlin are Jews. God be merciful to us poor Christians."

The popular University of Berlin history professor Heinrich von Treitschke added his prestige to the anti-Semitic surge. An ultranationalist, in an article for the *Preussische Jahrbücher* he insisted that Germany suffered from a "Jewish problem." Although a group of other academics, along with politicians and business leaders, responded in an open letter calling Treitschke's work a "disgrace," the Treitschke article included a phrase that has fueled anti-Semitic propaganda since: "The Jews are our misfortune." As recently as 2002, Treitschke continued to foment strife in Berlin. In comfortable Steglitz, a district in western Berlin, attempts were made by social activists to change the name of the street Treitschkestrasse to Kurt-Scharf-Strasse, after a Protestant leader who hid Jews from the Nazis. The Steglitz district council repeatedly rejected the appeals, and the street remains named after a public figure well remembered for calling Jews a "problem" and a "misfortune" for Germany.

Similar public slanders continued as Germany worked to rebuild its postcrash economy. Nonetheless, immigration from the East—where anti-Semitism was considered to be even worse— also continued. And, in another example of historical themes repeated in the current era, established and assimilated Jews in Berlin often expressed their own concerns about the influx of *Ostjuden*. A prime example is the (Jewish) industrialist and German foreign minister Walter Rathenau, who said of *Ostjuden*, "Strange sight! There in the midst of German life is an alien and isolated race of men. Loud and self-conscious in their dress, hot-blooded and restless in their manner. An Asiatic horde on the sandy plains of Prussia forming among themselves a closed corporation, rigorously shut off from the rest of the world. Thus they live half-willingly in their own ghetto, not a living limb of the people, but an alien organism of its body. So what is to be done? An event without historical precedent: the conscious effort of a race to adapt itself to alien conditions. The goal of the process should be, not imitation Germans, but Jews bred and educated as Germans." Rathenau considered himself the role model, saying, "I am a German of Jewish descent. My people is the German people, my fatherland is Germany, my religion that Germanic faith which is above all religions." His political career ended with his life when he was shot down in the streets of Berlin in 1922, targeted, the assassins later acknowledged, in part because he was a Jew.

Many longtime Jewish Berliners feared that anti-Semitism in their city would increase along with an increase in the Jewish population. These cosmopolitan and sophisticated city folk felt little affinity for their foreign country cousins. Of course, as the journalist Joseph Roth wrote in the twenties, "All Jews were once 'Eastern Jews,' before a few of them went West."

The theme keeps recurring. Note the words of General Count Friedrich Bernhard von der Schulenburg, on November 9, 1918, after the Treaty of Versailles ended World War I: "Our men will claim they were stabbed in the back by their comrades-at-arms, the navy, together with Jewish war profiteers and shirkers." In fact some 100,000 Jews served in the German army in World War I, 80,000 in front-line trenches. The army's own count determined that at least 10,000 Jewish German soldiers died for the Fatherland. A representative sampling of those graves can be seen in Berlin today at the Jewish cemetery in Weissensee.

During the twenties, Berlin filled with Russian expatriates seeking relief or refuge from the chaos of revolutionary Russia. By 1925, 160,000 *Ostjuden*, escaping from the chaos of Russia, were living in Prussia. Forty-four thousand of them were Berliners. One of them was Ilya Ehrenburg, who discovered quickly that a Russian could feel at home in some Berlin neighborhoods. "At every step, you could hear Russian spoken," he wrote. "Dozens of Russian restaurants were opened—with balalaikas and zurnas, with gypsies, pancakes, shashliks, and, naturally, the inevitable heartbreak. There was a little theatre that put on sketches. Three daily newspapers and five weeklies appeared in Russian. In one year seventeen Russian publishing firms were started." Ehrenburg could find a similar Berlin eighty years and another world war and cold war later.

One of those Russian newspapers was the daily *Prizyv*—The Calling. The paper was founded by a former tsarist army colonel, Fyodor Vinberg, who is credited with bringing some of the first copies of a fraud to Germany, a fraud that continues to foment anti-Semitism, *The Protocols of the Elders of Zion*. A tsarist intelligence officer named Rachkovsky is cited as responsible for creating the *Protocols* around 1895, a collection of manufactured documents that claims to report on secret meetings of the leadership of a worldwide Jewish conspiracy where decisions were made to gain world domination by overthowing all governments and religions. Vinberg used the pages of *Prizyv* to rail against Jews, specifically calling for genocide. "Vinberg was a true precursor of the Final Solution, even though at the time few paid attention to his ravings," writes *Protocols* expert Walter Laqueur.

In 1925 Adolf Hitler built on this long anti-Semitic history in what would become his global best-seller, *Mein Kampf*. "Without the clearest knowledge of the racial problem and hence the Jewish problem," he wrote, "there will never be a resurrection of the German nation." *Mein Kampf* continues to create controversy—and to attract readers. When I needed to refer to it for this book, I checked the extensive public library system in sophisticated Sonoma County, California, where I live. Almost every branch library here owns a copy. Every single copy was checked out. The popularity of Hilter's work among local library users didn't preclude my easy access to a copy: I found it for sale and in stock at the Borders bookstore just down the freeway in San Rafael. *Mein Kampf* remains restricted in Germany, technically forbidden for most of the German public to buy and sell. Scholars and journalists are permitted the right to use the book if they can prove a specific need acceptable to the government. A couple of choice quotes from this oft-cited book are reminders of the rhetoric Hitler used to punctuate his anti-Semitic arguments.

"Was there any form of filth or profligacy, particularly in cultural life, without at least one Jew involved in it? If you cut even cautiously into such an abscess, you found, like a maggot in a rotting body, often dazzled by the sudden light—a kike!"

Once the Nazis came to power in Germany, *Mein Kampf* was given as a wedding present to every newly married couple.

"With satanic joy in his face, the black-haired Jewish youth lurks in wait for the unsuspecting girl whom he defiles with his blood, thus stealing her from her people. With every means he tries to destroy the racial foundations of the people he has set out to subjugate. Just as he systematically ruins women and girls, he does not shrink back from pulling down the blood barriers for others, even on a large scale. It was and is the Jews who bring the Negroes into the Rhineland, always with the same secret thought and clear aim of ruining the hated white race by the necessarily resulting bastardization, throwing it down from its cultural and political height, and himself rising to be the master."

By 1935, with the Nazis well established in power, Hitler's raves became reality. Couples caught in relationships deemed inappropriate by the Nazis could expect to be forced to stand in the gutter holding placards drawing attention to their personal lives. An archival photograph from that year shows a blonde woman in heels and a stylish hat and frock with a sign hung from her neck reading, "I am the greatest swine and only get myself mixed up with Jews." Next to her is her man in a three-piece suit and a bow tie, holding a fedora and a sign that says, "I am a Jew, I only take German girls to my room."

In 1933 Jews were ordered to bring their passports to authorities for the addition of a "J" stamp. That same year all Jews living in Germany, but not born there, lost the right to apply for citizenship. "The nearly 150,000 Jews who were affected by this ruling had remained marginal to the Jewish community because of their poverty, their Yiddish language, and orthodox Jewish faith," writes the historian Claudia Koonz. "Assimilated Jews had often blamed these oddly dressed, uncouth newcomers for the hostility toward Jews in general, and did not become alarmed when their citizenship was voided."

Jews lost their civil rights one by one through the 1930s. *Kristallnacht* on November 9, 1938, the premeditated and systematic Nazi attack on Jews and their institutions and shops throughout Germany, left synagogues and stores in ruins, men and women dead, injured, and jailed. *Kristallnacht* convinced most Jews remaining in Germany that quitting the country was a priority. By the next year, about two-thirds of German Jews had emigrated. Many of those who stayed and became victims of the Nazis simply lacked the resources to leave and relocate.

Because of the integral role Jews had played in developing Berlin's culture and economy, by the twenties most had felt safely assimilated into the city's society. They had considered themselves Germans who merely happened to be Jewish. The Nazi crimes proved that this perceived assimilation was never complete.

5 □ *Berlin's Jewish Survivors*

OUTSIDE it is a rare perfect-weather Berlin day. I'm watching from our balcony in Schöneberg, one of Berlin's nicer neighborhoods. Birds are singing. The setting sun is lighting up clouds on their way to Poland, and the incoming weather looks clear. Down at the corner of Rosenheimer and Eisenacher, the Colombian waiter is chatting up a customer sitting outside at our local Italian restaurant, Chiaia. He's been here ten years and loves Berlin, where his drag-queen lifestyle isn't just tolerated, it's embraced. Someone somewhere is playing standards on a piano for the second evening in a row, and the music fills our corner. Across the street, two boys alternately pet and hit a leashed dog.

The routine of the corner is my routine now. I've been living in a fine apartment on Rosenheimerstrasse in a solid prewar block—high ceilings, hardwood floors, French doors connecting the airy rooms, ample windows to let in the light. The newsstand at the corner is open, and one by one anonymous neighbors stumble, stagger, stroll out of their flats to fetch a paper. A red Harley with a sidecar is parked up on the sidewalk, as usual. A white-haired man carrying his Sunday *Bild* walks past, stopping at the gutter to spit and scan the headlines.

Berlin is most quiet on Sunday mornings. I hear each car engine; footsteps are distinct; and now the church bells begin their reign on the morning—working up to their frenzied demand for attendance. I cross the street to look at the *Bild* headlines: always blood and scandal and sex, written in simple, declarative sentences.

The garbage truck is outside; the doorbell rings. In order for the garbagemen to get to the inside courtyard of the apartment building to collect the cans, they must pass through the main entrance door of the apartment house. This they accomplish by mercilessly ringing all the bells on the front panel early in the morning twice a week, expecting someone will buzz them into the lobby.

Mundane musings from my neighborhood, Schöneberg, a neighborhood that was home to many of the Jews who thrived in Berlin before the Third Reich. Perhaps its quiet routines help make an open-air memorial to anti-Semitism one of the most powerful I've witnessed. Banners hanging from the streetlamp posts simply recite the so-called Nuremberg Laws, one to a banner: no marriage between Jews and "Aryans," the ban against Jews working as domestics in non-Jewish households, no employment in journalism, no practicing law or medicine. Over fifty years later, the words look ridiculous, unbelievable. And terrifying when the context of their reality is remembered.

In 1936 CBS News correspondent William Shirer was not only reporting on the increasing number of laws restricting Jews, he was also noting the unofficial signs appearing at stores and on roadsides. "Jews Enter This Place at Their Own Risk" was one, and another, comical were it not for the malicious intent and the history that followed: "Drive Carefully! Sharp Curve! Jews 75 Miles an Hour!"

In those early days of official discrimination, the Nazi government struggled to identify exactly whom it was they hated. Their definitions of Jews were initially vague and convoluted. When Hitler first ordered his minions to outlaw intermarriage between so-called Aryans and Jews, there was no official definition of a Jew. No specific physiological characteristics were listed to identify Jews by the so-called racial experts in the Führer's employ. When the final Nuremberg Laws were announced, this formula was fixed: anyone with four grandparents who had been born Jewish was considered a Jew. As Claudia

Koonz points out in her book *Mothers in the Fatherland*, this ruling eliminated any legal argument about the existence of a Jewish race. Jewish identity, in the eyes of the Nazis, was based on the religious preference of grandparents. "By implication," she notes, "one could have eight great-grandparents who converted to Christianity and be considered 'Aryan.'" The newly created Office of Racial Affairs soon found itself struggling with further definitions. For example, it ruled that those with two grandparents who were not baptized were also Jews. "These categories," writes Koonz, "divided the Jewish community by offering slim hope to the fortunate *Mischlinge*," Jewish families that contained "Aryans."

In Germany these types of statistics on personal data were readily available to authorities. The law required (and still requires) all citizens to register with the police, a registration that includes noting religion. Foreigners too must register. When I first lived in Germany I remember well my shock at reading Question 12 on the *Anmeldung* form, the requirement to choose a religion from the two alternatives on the form: Protestant and Roman Catholic. The rationalization for this deeply personal inquiry was based on the fact that the state provided tax revenues directly to the churches for support, the amount of funding based on the numbers of followers. So the government needed to know how much money to disburse to the two major religions in Germany. If you were not Catholic or Protestant and wanted your tax money to go to another denomination, you were required to petition as an exception. A public denunciation of organized religion was required to avoid the church tax burden.

By 2002 sufficient numbers of Jews were again living in Germany to force a change in the law. The Central Council of German Jews and the chancellor's office finally concluded an agreement that provided Jewish religious institutions with legal status equal to that of the Protestant and Catholic churches. "The government wants to have a strong Jewish community," explained Chancellor Gerhard Schröder. The result was an increase in financing from public funds for institutions such as Jewish schools, an arrangement long enjoyed by Protestants and Catholics. The immediate effect was to triple the federal money available for Jews, to $3 million a year. The Central Council of German Jews earmarked the money to teach Judaism to nonreligious ethnic Jews newly arriving from the former Soviet bloc, and to train new rabbis.

This official effort to distinguish between some myth of a true German and the outsider—the foreigner—persists. *Washington Post* reporter Marc Fisher tells of discovering a particularly odd example during his posting in the nineties as the paper's bureau chief in Germany. "The German Interior Ministry repeatedly denied to me the existence of a form its border officials used to categorize people applying for residency in Germany. The form, used in several German states, required officials to note the shape of the applicant's nose. A German nose was described as 'normal'; a variety of codes were given for 'abnormal' nose shapes found in other parts of the world. When an official finally conceded the existence of the form, he called it 'routine.'"

The Israeli journalist Yaron Svoray encountered the nose question when he was researching a book about neo-Nazis in Germany and posing as a sympathizer with the neo-Nazi movement. Here is an excerpt from his story, which he tells in the third person, as he tries to infiltrate a group that calls itself the Free German Workers' party in Cologne.

"We want a free Europe. A white Europe," said one.

"What's a white Europe?" asked Svoray.

"Where other races are sent back, to their roots. Some persons with big noses back to . . ."

"Who are the ones with the big noses? The Jews?"

"Yes, the Jews. I'm looking at your nose. I'm not sure

about you." This stopped the conversation. The speaker was a blond young man with cold eyes. "Has anyone looked at his credentials?" He stared from face to face around the room.

Svoray jumped to his feet. "Are you saying I have a Jewish nose? Those are fighting words, my friend."

Laughter defused the moment, to Svoray's relief.

Defining who is a Jew remains problematic, even in the United States. Recent attempts to conduct a census of the American Jewish population were confused by attempts to ascertain what in fact constitutes a Jew. The Institute for Jewish and Community Relations considers Jews not only those who identify themselves as practicing Jews but also people who say they were Jewish but now follow other religions; those who call themselves ethnically or culturally Jewish but do not follow a religion; those who follow no religion but who were raised as Jews or had a Jewish parent. The National Jewish Population Survey, sponsored by the United Jewish Communities, is somewhat more restrictive, adding to those who identify themselves as Jews only those who claim no religion but were raised as Jews or had a Jewish parent.

BERLIN HAS HAD a long history as a refuge for people escaping persecution elsewhere in Europe. But Adolf Hitler and the Nazis interrupted that history with twelve years of war and state-sponsored mass murder. By the time the Russian army took Berlin and the Allies won the war in Europe, the Holocaust had killed 6 million European Jews and in the process destroyed Germany's vibrant Jewish community. Before the war, 160,000 of Germany's half-million Jews lived in Berlin. Only a few thousand survived in Hitler's capital, hidden and fed by courageous Christian Germans risking their own lives.

After the Nazis invaded Poland in 1939, they inaugurated the mass murder of Jews, made more efficient with the establishment of the concentration cum extermination camp at

Auschwitz in 1940. Finally in 1942, at the Wannsee conference in Berlin, the highest-ranking Nazis designed their Final Solution, the planned extermination of most Jews. There were exceptions made for certain categories of German Jews based on age, extraordinary military service in World War I, and some of those from families with mixed heritage.

Berlin's prewar Jewish population of some 160,000 was already diminished by about half once the war began. Enforcement of the Nuremberg Laws made it difficult to earn a living, and after *Kristallnacht* in 1938, German Jews were forced to acknowledge the physical danger they faced in their daily activities from Nazi officials and thugs on the street. Many chose to emigrate. But other Jews resettled to Berlin from the rest of Germany, hoping to survive in the anonymity of the still relatively tolerant population.

Deportations of Berlin Jews to Auschwitz began in late 1941. Six months later, on May 11, 1942, a well-informed estimate of the size of the community comes from an entry in Joseph Göbbels's diary. "There are still 40,000 Jews in Berlin and despite the heavy blows dealt them they are still insolent and aggressive. It is exceedingly difficult to shove them off to the East because a large part of them are at work in the munitions industry and because the Jews are to be evacuated only by families." Later that year the Jewish workforce was replaced with foreign laborers from conquered territories. On February 27, 1943, the Nazis attempted to arrest the 25,000 or so Jews still living in Berlin. A frustrated Göbbels figured that about 4,000 escaped the SS troops assigned to capture them. Many of those managed to survive the war, some taking advantage of loopholes in the Nazi laws, others living underground, and a few acting as "catchers" who worked for the Nazis identifying other Jews hiding in Berlin.

Other estimates of the number of survivors differ. Claudia Koonz estimates that about twenty thousand German Jews refused to wear the yellow star and became so-called *U-boots*, referred to as submarines, and lived underground. She figures that about two-thirds survived the war. The office of the Berlin government responsible for Jewish affairs stated in 1947 that five thousand Jews were successfully hidden by Berliners during the Nazi era.

Horst Gessner is one of those survivors. We meet on a sunny winter day in his apartment on the east side of Berlin. This cheery pensioner is waiting for me with paraphernalia from his war years in Berlin spread on his living room table: several Nazi-era identity papers and a tattered and dirty Star of David, black outlined on yellow fabric with the word "Jude" printed through the middle of the star. Gessner all but threw the yellow star onto the table with disgusted dismissal, despite the fact that he had saved the relic all these years.

I ask him what he was thinking while he was displaying the star. "To describe my feelings is very difficult," he tells me, "because, just taking this in my hand for me always means thinking of the past, and the past of course in my case, and for hundreds of thousands of other Jewish citizens in Germany, in Berlin, was not exactly pleasant during the Nazi era."

The dark black hair that appears in the pictures of the young Horst Gessner on the old identity papers is now a distinguished-looking silver. His eyes are bright, his answers lucid, thoughtful, and thorough.

"I have to thank my father for this," he says about his survival in Berlin through the war years. "My father was, according to the legislation of the Nazis—I have to use their wording now—'Aryan by race.' My mother was Jewish, fully Jewish, from a religious Jewish home. In accordance with the wishes of both parents, I became at birth a member of the Jewish community, complete with the entire ritual—that is, circumcision—as was customary for Jews." His father did more than just accept his wife's religion. "My father also converted to Judaism, also with the entire ritual that was customary for Jews." But by the strange laws created by the Nazis, the father's conversion did not make him a Jew. Since the father's familial heritage was Christian, the Nazis simply did not recognize the conversion. "For the Nazis, religious affiliation did not matter, only race."

Consequently the Gessner family was not immediately targeted for deportation. As was the case with so many other German Jews, they watched the deterioration of their country with a certain amount of complacency. "There was in Germany, also in my family, always this feeling: It's not going to be that bad. The Nazis won't be able to stay in power that long. But of course they did stay in power for twelve years until they were, for the time being at least, swept off the face of the earth." A rueful smile. "My father was exposed to a lot of pressures, was summoned to appear before the Gestapo, summoned to the police, always with many offers to separate from his Jewish wife. But that would have meant immediate deportation to the extermination camps [for Horst and his mother]. As long as my father stood by the marriage, we were protected from deportation. Not from harassment, but from deportation. Thus it was life preserving." He nods his head in memory.

While thousands and thousands of Jews were rounded up and deported east to concentration and extermination camps, Gessner lived in Berlin as a Jew, protected by the bizarre definitions the Nazis devised to identify Jews. The capriciousness of the distinctions made by the Nazis, the arbitrary reality of their edicts, saved him while others were killed.

"That's how it is." Gessner closes his eyes and nods again as he explains his strange status. "According to the so-called Nuremberg Laws, the Reichs Law for the Protection of the German Blood, I was regarded as—this is the Nazi term—as a 'recognized Jew.' As a 'recognized Jew' I had to be equipped with a Jewish identification card, I had to have the middle name—the forcibly ordered middle name—'Israel.' My mother had to have the middle name 'Sara,' and on our front door was—so that everyone could see it—just like this yellow Jewish star, a Jewish star in white, but otherwise in appearance and size exactly like it. And under this sign, affixed to the apartment door, the names of those household members who were Jewish, so in our case: Horst Israel Gessner, Gözi Sara Gessner."

Throughout the war the two of them remained protected by the luck of her earlier marriage. "Yes, until 1945. The Nazis did a lot of harassment, but they did not force a divorce on anyone, they did not do that." With other Jews surviving through the Final Solution because of similar loopholes, the family maintained some sense of community. "We had a lot of contact. Hard times bind people together. Necessity is the mother of invention. For example, my father was a tailor." Gessner's eyes start to brighten, he smiles and laughs at the memory he's about to share, a full and happy-sounding laugh. "He prepared the Jewish star with a unique attachment. It was sewn onto a small piece of fabric, and was fastened to our clothes with a hook on a chain, so you could detach it anytime. But as clever as we were, the Nazis of course were no less so. At control points they always looked to see if the star was solid or detachable, for it had to be sewed on securely." The smile is gone.

The "Aryan" background of Horst's father offered no protection outside the immediate family. "We had of course, as long as this was still possible, contact with my mother's family. It caused her great suffering: her brother, his wife, her sister with her husband, another sister with a daughter were all deported, all gassed to death, no one came back." A deep sigh. "Thanks to the death lists of the Nazis, which are available from the Jewish community, we were able to find out into which extermination camps they were put, and perished." And now there are tears in Gessner's eyes as he remembers and politely listens for my next question.

It must be difficult to relive these times, I say in response to the tears, and I make it clear that I appreciate his sharing his stories so others can learn from his experiences.

"My mother, naturally, was a member of the Jewish community until her death," he continues. She had no choice. But Gessner's parents thought there might be an alternative for him. "I left the Jewish community. I have to say, I was made to go, because my parents did it for me, on the false assumption that if I were taken out of the Jewish community I would not have to wear the Jewish star. But that was a false assumption. The Nazis, as I said, went according to race." Religious conversion was no protection if the Nazis were aware of the past. Nonetheless Horst Gessner became a Christian of convenience. "I was ten years old, baptized in St. Sophie's Church as a Lutheran. The pastor there knew that what he did was punishable by law, but he baptized Jewish citizens as Protestants. With that I had an additional document to present at control points, my baptism document." As long as the officials who stopped him did not check carefully, he could pass as a Christian and take advantage of opportunities as basic as buying the kinds of groceries not available to Jews in Berlin.

When the war finally ended, Gessner found himself in the Russian-occupied zone, where he continued to live until the city reunified. "With the fall of the Wall, all of us were given the opportunity to reestablish relationships between both parts of the city, which had, after all, been separated arbitrarily." He shrugs his shoulders and adds that this reconciliation resulted in new conflicts and problems between the Jews of East and West Berlin. "But that's normal." He's delighted by the exodus to Berlin from the former Soviet bloc and the resurgence of the Jewish community. "We were really all very happy about it, everyone in my circle of friends, that Jewish citizens from other countries—the former Soviet Union, and Poland, Hungary, Romania—could immediately come to Germany. But in my opinion there is a lot of built-in conflict in this offer, 'Come to Germany.' How are these citizens received and treated in Germany? For example, as Russian Jews they were never particularly welcome in Russia, whether that was tsarist Russia, or later under Soviet power, or now in the new Russia. They were always second-class citizens there. They came here thinking that this is now their country. But in principle they are second-class citizens here too, because they are now regarded as foreigners, and the Germans—well, they've got a thing about foreigners."

Horst Gessner shakes his head. "It is is awful. It fills me with anger and rage when I see that, after so much horror, such horror can happen again in Germany. But it can be stopped. I am all for democracy, but the democracy must also be able to detain people who despise democracy, and show them limits and borders, and not only through a demonstration." He is referring to the massive march in the streets of Berlin on November 9, 2000, billed as a march for tolerance. "And not only through forbidding a political party. That is correct, that is important, but that is only one device." He is referring to the attempts by the government to outlaw the right-wing National Democratic party, the NPD. He worries that the government's response is weak and ineffective. "One must also use all means of the state to destroy these rightist extremists who are gaining strength again. I don't mean physically destroy them, but destroy their organizations."

But Gessner acknowledges with frustration that problems for the new immigrants come not just from the extreme right. Some established German Jews are not happy with the new influx of Jewish immigrants from the East. "I don't want to make any judgments, that is not for me to do, but opinion within the Jewish community is not uniform. Jewish community members are part of the whole German people, and in the community you hear a lot of this: 'What do these people want here now?' That is not a new thing, for in earlier years there was always a difference in the Jewish community between the German Jews and the Polish Jews, for example."

Berlin, of course, is not the only place where conflicts and resentments between longtime Jewish residents and new Jewish immigrants have caused problems within the Jewish community. New York is another good example. "Yes, there were very strong differences. You have them in Israel as well, between the strictly orthodox and the liberal Jews. The Jewish community has great difficulties."

Gessner tells stories of Jews hesitant to study the German language in classes offered at the public schools, worried about harassment there. This fear adds another burden, he says, to the Jewish community, which feels compelled to organize its own classes to teach the new immigrants in a protected environment. He recites the types of taunts he's told that the newcomers hear from their classmates:

"Oh, where are you from?"

"Foreigners we've got enough, now we have to have you guys too!"

Many Germans, he says, express social exhaustion:

"Leave us alone with this! Leave us in peace, the Nazi time is past!"

And some, he says, are harsher with their words:

"Well, you Jewish citizens, you have received enough from the state. What more do you want now?"

Considering what he personally experienced through the Nazi era, combined with the resurgence of anti-Semitism during the current period of Jewish immigration, I ask Horst Gessner if he feels there is a stable and secure future for a Jewish community in Germany. "My personal opinion—and that's the only one I can express—is that it would be wrong to say Jewish citizens have no future in Germany, because that is exactly what the rightists want. No. One must not give up without a fight. Jewish citizens themselves must be active in creating conditions that will allow them to live here in peace and quiet and, above all, in safety." Not only the Jews, he says, but all foreigners who immigrate to Germany must take an active role in protecting themselves and in building a civil society. At the same time, it is not enough for the government to take responsibility just for food and housing. "One has to give the immigrants work. If they have no job, they become second-class citizens, with the attitude, 'I am not needed' or 'I am not allowed to work.' It is, of course, a question of earning one's own money," Gessner says about the crucial value of self-esteem.

He leans back in his comfortable easy chair, surrounded by the accoutrements of a contented existence in his modest but comfortable apartment. This man is remarkably relaxed and open-minded given the hardships and miseries of German history he's lived through, first under Hitler's terror, then under the East German Communist dictatorship, and now in the midst of the changes resulting from German unification. Who are you? I ask him. Are you a German? Are you a citizen of a state that no longer exists? Are you a Jew?

The question evokes a tight smile. "A very difficult question. First of all, I have difficulties with the question, What is my home country?" He says it again, using the phraseology, *Was ist mein Heimatland*. And *Heimatland* translates culturally to a different meaning than the literal words "home country" or "homeland." Perhaps *Heimatland* in American English is closer to "hometown," that sense of the place whence one comes and where one feels one belongs. Gessner speaks slowly as he makes an attempt at describing his identity. "Because this *Heimatland* was split not only by the Wall but above all by attitudes. Humanism was interpreted differently by everyone. I must say that in 1945—this happens to be the way it is—we were freed by Russian troops." Gessner and his family were as happy to see the Russians in Berlin as Parisians were to see the Americans. "My mother, my father, as well as I, we smothered them with our embraces, because they were seriously our liberators. That is a fact. Of course they were a part of the Allies, clearly."

But the family initially was regarded as suspect. "At first we had difficulties making it clear that we were Jews, because among the Soviets the news had spread, justifiably: 'There cannot be any Jews left here! You are lying, you are Nazis!'" The liberators summoned Jewish officers from their ranks. "My mother had to recite the Kaddish. She was able to do it, whereas I would have had difficulties with it." A wide smile. "And with that, everything was fine. They heaped—I don't want to say where they got it—but they heaped food and other goods on us and everything one needs."

They also put Horst Gessner to work, ordering him to organize an "anti-fascist democratic youth" group in his neighborhood, Prenzlauerberg. "I had absolutely no idea where to start. But it was logical. They knew that youth needed to be given something to do. For the youth especially, an entire world collapsed with the collapse of Nazism." Gessner's non-Nazi background made him ideal for the work. "I very much enjoyed doing that, along with some Jewish friends who survived. We here in the DDR,* when the DDR here was founded in 1949, we didn't have a special Jewish problem."

But with the demise of the DDR, who is he now?

"I see myself as a German citizen who is, without being a member of the Jewish community, strongly rooted in Judaism, based on my entire history." And he returns to that history, acknowledging that mistakes were made in the DDR. "But what was done in regard to the victims of National Socialism, I must say, that was first-class." Unification after the Wall fell, he also applauds, calling it "a happy hour for the German people."

His humility continues as he talks about himself in historical context. So I interrupt and ask again, Who are you? He nods and smiles and sums up his autobiography. "A human being who feels good, who never forgets his past, nor will deny it. I will also not deny my life in the DDR. I did not choose it. I was, so to speak, born into it, put into it." He looks content with acceptance as he describes those years in the discredited country. "I harbor no hatred against the DDR, not at all, but naturally no

---

*The Deutsche Demokratische Republik, the German Democratic Republic, was the official name of East Germany.

hatred either against the new regime, toward which I feel greatly indebted. I am very involved in this regime. I know that I have many, many democratic rights in this system, many even that I did not have before. But I also know that one has to fight for these rights, and that the people in government—no matter which kind—always need a little fire put under their butts, so that they don't just sit but also comprehend that they must keep their promises." He laughs. "Before elections a lot is always promised, not only in Germany but in other countries as well."

Before we say goodbye, one by one he shows me his old Nazi documents and describes them.

The first shows him as still a young boy. The cover page of a tattered piece of paper features a huge "J" in the old-style Gothic German script. "This document is the identification card. Practically every Reichs German had an ID card, but this identification card was one for Jewish citizens. It was marked with the 'J,' for 'Jude.'" He opens the paper. Inside is his picture affixed with rivets and stamped with the Nazi eagle and swastika. Next to his picture are his fingerprints. "Here was also the name: Horst Israel Gessner," he points to Israel, the name the Nazis added. "Documents had to be shown at every visit to the authorities, and immediately it was apparent: the bearer of this card was a Jew."

Gessner next takes the soiled Star of David in his hands, calling it "a stigma for a German state, home of Goethe, Schiller, Heine, to make such a marking for human beings, and with it declare them outlaws."

As Gessner grew through his teenage years during the Nazi era, his identity papers changed. "Every citizen who was approaching his eighteenth birthday had to appear before the draft board in order to be evaluated for the military, and before that possibly for the labor service. One received a summons, one had to go the district office of the military, there were the usual examinations, and then the relevant documents. I was excluded from the district labor service. I was not mad about it—reason:

Jew." And he shows off another document written in the discredited Gothic script* and filled with swastikas and eagles.

Still another Nazi document from 1944 "shows that I was permanently excluded from service in the fascist military. All other citizens received a military pass; I received an exclusion document. During the Nazi period it was difficult to get through controls with such documents. When the Soviets were here it was a credential to prove that I could never have been in the fascist military." Here he is pictured as a handsome young man in a jacket and tie, the same wavy hair piled high. "It is an exclusion document from the military. It says who was unworthy."

All these years later, what are his feelings holding these mementos of such ghastly times?

"Contradictory," he says without hesitation. "On the one hand, I was glad not to be in the fascist military. On the other hand, this was always a very, very dangerous document, because during the war there were civil patrols, military patrols, and one always had to show documents, and to show this document without wearing the Jewish star meant deportation."

IMMEDIATELY after the war ended, Germany briefly became an ironic destination for Jews liberated in Eastern Europe and panicked about resurging anti-Semitism in Poland, Romania, Hungary, and other countries east of Germany. They created a short-term exodus to Berlin and Germany, filling Displaced Persons camps. There they waited while they hoped for visas and transport on to British-controlled Palestine, or whatever safe haven would take them. In 1946 there were 72 of the DP camps in Austria, Germany, and Italy, filled with some 250,000 Jews struggling to survive on minimal rations provided by the Allies. Most eventually resettled in the late forties in newly independent Israel.

*The black-letter typeface is associated with its use by the Nazis. Because of this connotation, it is rarely used in contemporary Germany even though its use in printing dates from Gutenberg's early movable type.

6 □ *Who Is a Jew?*

IT IS DAYBREAK at Germany's border with Poland, in the state of Brandenburg, town of Peitz. This crisp and clear winter morning in January 2001 is the first sunrise in the new life of a Jewish family, the Rojsenblats, just arrived from Ukraine. The Rojsenblats are one more Jewish family from the former Soviet Union joining the exodus of Jews to Germany. This father, mother, and son are three of the tens of thousands of Jewish immigrants who are running to refuge in Germany from religious persecution, violence, and economic chaos.

The German government operates several reception centers designed to assist these immigrants. The Rojsenblats arrive at the Landestelle für Aussiedler—the state government office for resettlement—located in a nondescript Communist-era block building on the edge of Peitz, on Juri-Gagarin-Strasse. The street is named in honor of the Soviet cosmonaut. For the immigrants it's both a reminder of home and of the cold war years when the Soviets subjugated East Germany. In one of the upstairs office suites, the Rojsenblats sit around a conference table with two German government officials and a translator as they exchange their Soviet-era Ukrainian passports, an example of documents that specifically identify "nationality" as "Jew," for German papers, and for what they hope and expect is a better life in Germany.

In a businesslike manner the Germans explain the details of the family's changing status. Mother Irma is fixed with a serious look on her face, but after father Vladimir signs the family's paperwork renouncing allegiance to Ukraine and embracing Germany, he smiles, his lips tight together. It's a subtle and restrained smile, but his eyes give away more emotion. They are bright with pleasure. "In one sentence," he explains his motives, "I can say we seek security and a safe future for our son. That's what it's about."

Eighteen-year-old Alexandr agrees enthusiastically. "I was in Germany before, for one year as an exchange student. So I know this country and, yeah. I feel happy. It's a new step in my life. It will be difficult, but I think I will handle it."

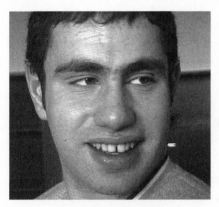

Alexandr Rojsenblat

Alexandr studied in Kiev at a Jewish school where he heard from others about their experiences with anti-Semitism. "I didn't face it, but I didn't want to wait to face it," he says. Stories about skinheads and neo-Nazis in Germany don't worry him much. "In Ukraine we have a lot of skinheads too. Not a lot," he corrects himself, "but we have them."

I ask him about his identity. What will he be in this new life? A Ukrainian? A Jew? A German?

Alexandr smiles and pauses to think about the question.

"I don't know. We'll see. I think I will be a Jew, first of all." He hesitates. Then he announces with confidence and vigor, "I will be a German Jew!"

The Rojsenblats are on their way to their new home living with relatives in the Berlin suburb of Potsdam. For Jewish immigrants without funds or family support, the German government provides relocation services. After as few as five days in clean, warm, but cramped reception-center quarters such as those in Peitz, the newcomers are scattered across the country. During their stay at the Landestelle für Aussiedler, the children play in well-equipped kindergartens while German-language classes are held for the adults. In one room the middle-aged students sit around a table with their teacher, a stack of Russian-German dictionaries, and copies of clippings from the local newspapers. The day the Rojsenblats become German citizens, in a classroom down the hall from where they signed the papers other Russian speakers are laboring through a news story about the weather in Siberia—another reason to be glad for the move to Germany. "I have seen birds in flight die from the cold," reads the headline.

Living quarters are tight, families crowded into rooms barely large enough to accommodate a couple of bunk beds, a tiny table, and a mini-refrigerator, oven, and range. The building is sparkling clean.

Once resettled, some of the newcomers are lucky enough to land in cosmopolitan cities while others are placed by the government in remote German villages far from any established Jewish community.

Alexandr Rojsenblat, the fresh-faced immigrant from Ukraine, says he will be a German Jew. But what exactly is a German Jew? Who makes that definition and how? The answer speaks to the core of the unrelenting problems Germans face in dealing with their past, to the present influx of Jews immigrating to Germany, and to the future of German society.

Shortly after Alexandr Rojsenblat came to Germany, the elected leader of the German Jewish community, Paul Spiegel, added his voice to the centuries-long attempts to define Germans and Jews. Spiegel used his position as president of the Central Council of Jews in Germany to announce that he feared some thirty thousand of the immigrants arriving in Germany since the fall of the Wall who claimed to be Jewish in order to get citizenship, were not. Spiegel worried that these posers simply added to Germany's growing social problems because so many were economic refugees and immediately sought and received government support. He told the world that many of the newcomers did not pass Halachic religious laws tests for being Jewish and that bona fide German Jews ought to work alongside Interior Ministry officials in German embassies to determine which applicants for entry to the country claiming to be Jewish really were Jewish.

The Interior Ministry dismissed Spiegel's concerns, insisting that its consuls adequately check all the stories told to them at visa offices, and that they are in an ideal position to determine which applicants are bona fide Jews.

The Russian comedian Wladimir Kaminer knows Paul Spiegel is correct about such imposters. They are part of Kaminer's act. He moved to Berlin from Moscow in 1990 in that first wave of Eastern Europeans who headed toward Berlin just after the Wall fell.

"The new era dawned," he remembers. "Now the free ticket to the big wide world, the invitation to make a fresh start, was yours if you were Jewish. Jews who had formerly paid to have the word 'Jew' removed from their passports now started shelling out to have it put in."

In the confusion—the revolution—following the fall of the Wall, laws changed quickly in both East and West Germany. The gates of Berlin opened once again for Jews, this time not only with absolutely no restrictions but with a most generous social welfare package to aid in successful resettlement.

"At that time no one could understand why the Germans were choosing to accept us, of all people," is how Wladimir Kaminer interprets those fast-moving events he and so many others took advantage of. "Perhaps police headquarters on Alexanderplatz had misunderstood something when they processed the first Jews, got it wrong, and ever since the worthy officers had been carrying on regardless, rather than admit their mistake? Much as they did when the Wall came down?"

Kaminer is right; that's basically how the first Jews slipped through the system. The Soviet Union was collapsing from the radical changes brought about by Mikhail Gorbachev's *perestroika* and *glasnost*. The resulting return of overt anti-Semitism in Russia and the other Soviet republics coincided with the general confusion of the revolutionary times. Travel restrictions were dropped or difficult to enforce. Jews made the relatively quick and easy trip to East Germany and sought help and asylum from the East Berlin authorities. On July 11, 1990, the East German government—as one of its reforms after its Communist dictatorship imploded—passed a law ensuring sanctuary in East Germany for the arriving Jewish refugees. Once in East Berlin, it was an easy walk for many of the incoming Jews across what just a few months before had been the Wall and into the more attractive West Berlin.

After German reunification on September 12, 1990, the East German sanctuary policy for Jews was codified for the entire nation. The law simply states that "people who fulfill the definition of Jewish origin receive an immigration permit." The German statute explains that it uses Jewish religious laws to define who is a Jew. "Immigrants must have a Jewish mother or must have converted according to rabbinical law." German consular offices in the former Soviet republics are charged with vetting applications to ensure that those claiming to be Jews meet the established criteria. Consular officers are instructed by law to cross-check their findings with the Jewish community's official authorities in Germany. That's the point in the law that Paul Spiegel wishes to use as a rationale for his office working more closely with the Interior Ministry to check applicants.

The law further mandates that German-language courses be made available at no cost to the immigrants while they wait for their paperwork to be processed. Those who drafted the law understood the problems these newcomers would face. They ordered that the immigrants be counseled about integration into German society and that they be resettled in places where Jewish communities already exist, or at least close to such communities. "Immigration of Jews from the former Soviet Union is guaranteed," the law unequivocally states, adding that "the goal is for permanent growth of Jewish communities in Germany."

How to define what constitutes being a Jew is neatly addressed in an essay by New York University communications professor Douglas Rushkoff, who rejects the notion of a Jewish race. "The very notion of a Jewish race was conceived in persecution and galvanized in extermination," he writes. "As a Jew who cares deeply about his religion, I have come to the conclusion that our great mistake has been to forget that we are the descendants of a loose amalgamation of peoples united around a new idea, and to replace this history with the view, advanced by our enemies, that we are a race."

"There are three ways of becoming a Jew: by birth, by conversion, by decree," writes the historian Peter Gay, explaining that he was "forcibly enlisted in the third group" by the Nazis. "We were Germans," Gay remembers in his memoir of his years as a boy in Nazi-controlled Berlin. "The gangsters who had taken control of the country were not Germany—we were."

7 □ *Emigrants Long for a German Visa*

IMMIGRATION TO GERMANY is excruciatingly difficult for most of the desperate hopefuls worldwide who see Germany as one of the most attractive destinations for political sanctuary and economic opportunity. In addition to Jews from the former Soviet Union, two other groups have enjoyed the privileges of instant German citizenship. Before the disintegration of East Germany, any East German who made his or her way over the Wall immediately would be granted full civil rights in the West. The West German Basic Law, the constitution written with guidance from the occupying Allies, guaranteed Federal Republic citizenship for Germans no matter which side they happened to be on when the country was divided.

This was an easy policy to advertise as long as the East Germans forced their people to stay put, creating few burdens for the West while providing the West with a terrific propaganda tool that made it appear to be a champion of human rights.

The other category of immigrant to Germany that receives this fast-track treatment is so-called ethnic Germans who are born outside Germany but are citizens of other nations. Before the fall of Eastern European communism, this was another valuable public relations tool. The West German government looked and acted heroic as it accepted the trickle of immigrants with German ancestors who managed to make their way out of the Soviet bloc. I watched at the Friedland refugee camp as a

Polish family made their appeal to become Germans. The wife did the talking; the husband's command of the German language was poor. She told the investigating immigration officer some family stories and produced some tattered photographs of relatives, along with some faded documents suggesting family lineage connected with Germany. It was enough. They received their *Stempel*, their official stamp, and their new papers announcing them as Germans. After a few more days in the dormitory of the camp, they would be off to new life as born-again Germans.

A seemingly endless trail of dirt-poor Mexicans labor north and across the U.S.-Mexico border carrying with them an important piece of common knowledge: If their baby is born in the United States, American citizenship is an immediate and automatic guarantee. American law and the spirit of the Melting Pot mandate that everyone and anyone—no matter the status of the parents—born in the U.S.A. is an American.

In Europe, while Germany acts as the same type of immigration magnet for the poor and the oppressed as the United States does in the New World, there is no line at the Polish border of Eastern Europeans scurrying across the Oder River with the expectation of creating a next generation of German citizens for the family. If a baby is born on German national territory, the place of birth means merely a German city name on the birth certificate, not citizenship. German law, like that of much of Europe, insists that nationality is determined by blood: the nationality of the parents. Or even grandparents. Or great-grandparents.

When I propose to Germans that the American Melting Pot is a more appropriate model, I'm often mocked. "Your melting pot is in your head," I've been told over and over. "America is not a happy, homogeneous society," they insist.

Immigration reform is in Germany's future. Shouts of protest continue that Germany is not an immigrant society, but it must accommodate immigration to survive. Its population is aging, and its birthrate is too low to maintain a viable workforce. A 2001 German federal government immigration study made reality official with its summary: "Germany needs immigrants." Despite this obvious conclusion, granting citizenship to those *Ausländers*—more than seven million foreigners already live in the country—continues to be a difficult jump for many Germans to make. Yet the nation embraces as Germans those emigrants who left the Fatherland generations ago.

Consider Gerta Rothermel. She saw Germany for the first time in the springtime of her seventy-seventh year, as she landed in Berlin from Moscow and was greeted with German citizenship, food, housing, and a cash allowance. I visit her in the sparse room she shares with three other so-called ethnic Germans in an East Berlin resettlement home.

It is a fresh day in Berlin, just a couple of months after Frau Rothermel's arrival. The window of her room is wide open, the birds are singing loudly, the grounds around the home are lush and green as she relives her Soviet misery.

"I have a difficult past," says Frau Rothermel as she pulls out a looseleaf binder filled with the official and family documents that proved to the German embassy in Moscow that she qualified for repatriation. Her hair is snow white, her face covered with canyonlike wrinkles, her teeth few and jagged. She fingers what seems to her to be the most important piece of paper in the stack. "Dear Mrs. Rothermel," she reads it slowly, in German. "Your father, Andrew, born 1877, was arrested on December 15, 1937, and was executed on January 9, 1938. Unfortunately, the place of burial is not known."

The letter acknowledging her father's execution helped Frau Rothermel prove that she was eligible for the largesse of Article 116 of the German constitution, the "Right of Return" law. It promises German citizenship to millions of ethnic Germans—and their descendants—who emigrated east to Russia, Poland, and Romania since the late 1700s and then suffered in their new homelands because they were Germans. The law was a comfortable piece of propaganda as long as the Iron Curtain was in place. The postwar German government could appear accommodating, safe in the knowledge that few of those millions would be allowed to leave their Soviet bloc homes. With the freedom to travel that came with the end of Eastern European and Soviet communism beginning in 1989, the trail west was packed with immigrants hoping to prove German heritage. The German government instituted an annual cap of 220,000 returnees. Nonetheless, at a time of high taxes, a depressed economy, and escalating unemployment, the "Right of Return" law remained a domestic political issue. Chancellor Helmut Kohl supported it as a device to keep in touch with nationalistic German voters; the opposition Social Democrats tried to attract more pragmatic voters with their campaign to cut the annual quota of incoming ethnic Germans in half.

Like many of German descent from Russia, Frau Rothermel was born along the Volga River. The tsars invited industrious Germans with their agricultural expertise to develop the region, promising them the good life in Russia. But when the Stalin-Hitler partnership turned sour, Frau Rothermel and her friends and family were banished to Kazakhstan and initially locked up in camps. "My whole youth, I spent my whole life there," she laments about her Central Asian exile. "My husband got killed too. He was in the camp for fifteen years. Millions got shot." It was 1969 before she was allowed to leave Kazakhstan. "I couldn't get out. We had nothing. We had to work, but who wanted to work there? Sometimes there were such snowstorms that people had to bind themselves together with cords. And the air was so bad."

Eventually she made her way to Moscow and an education, became a civil engineer, worked and retired. When the opportunity to leave Russia became real for her, she began assembling the paperwork needed to prove to the German authorities that she—despite her place of birth—is a German. "When one wants to come to Germany," she explains, "one must prove one's past."

After securing death certificates, birth certificates, and official stamps, and filling out detailed German government forms, she joined the long lines at the German embassy in Moscow, intent on proving that she was a displaced member of the tribe. "I am a German. My mentality is German," she says authoritatively, adding that she knows Goethe, loves Mozart.

Finally Frau Rothermel's application was approved. She said a quick goodbye, with no misgivings, to Moscow—and climbed onto the jet to Berlin. "From Moscow to here with such a good airplane!" she reports with girlish enthusiasm. "I came to Germany and everybody treated me like part of the family. I felt immediately so free and so good. I got a room and money. Look how people here are, not only to me—but to anybody! I am very satisfied and thankful."

Frau Rothermel is understandably thankful, but she is wrong: Germany certainly does not treat every newcomer equally. Younger immigrants from Russia and the former Central Asian Soviet republics find themselves struggling in the highly competitive German job market. More than two million ethnic Germans made the pilgrimage back to Deutschland in the first dozen years after the Soviet Union fell apart, many of them in the prime of their working years. For these new arrivals—who often speak little or no German and who face the culture shock of moving from a primitive rural to a modern urban environment—the adjustment is much tougher than the homecoming retirement enjoyed by Frau Rothermel.

"In Kazakhstan they said we were Germans and should go back to Germany," a thirty-something librarian underemployed in western Germany told the *New York Times*. "Now we are in Germany and the people here curse us as the Russians."

Sixteen-year-old Nikolai Kusnezov ended up on the wrong side of a barroom brawl in Weisswasser, a depressed city in the eastern Germany rustbelt. "As the guy walked away," Kusnezov told a *Los Angeles Times* reporter, "I heard him call me a 'dirty

Russian.'" Kusnezov was born in Kazakhstan, but he too is ethnically German, welcomed back by authorities once his family proved its German heritage. Despite this ancestry, he's considered a foreigner by the local gangs of undereducated and unemployed loiterers. "When I first arrived, the Germans called us dirty Russians. They told me to go away and they beat me. The neo-Nazis came after me. I couldn't do anything. But one day I decided to get my friends and get revenge. There were thirty of us. We told the neo-Nazis to meet us at the stadium by the Esso station. Fifty Nazis showed up. We beat each other up. We had fists. They had bats. We won anyway, and now the Nazis leave us alone."

The German government, trying to deal with rising unemployment exacerbating the social problems already faced and caused by young Nikolai and his peers, responded by finally making immigration more difficult for the *Aussiedler*—Germans call these long-lost relatives "resettlers." Now they must prove some German-language proficiency. In addition the German government is providing foreign aid money to ethnic Germans who choose to stay in the former Soviet republics where they were born.

MORE THAN seven million foreigners with no German heritage in their families live legally in Germany. Many of them seek German citizenship or just a continuing relationship with the country. For these immigrants, the realities of German law and custom present difficult barriers and hurdles, and are often just plain bizarre. For example, the blood-based German citizenship law gives automatic citizenship to a child born to a married couple if one of the parents is German. If that child is born out of wedlock, it is recognized by law as a German citizen if the mother is German. If only the poor bastard's father is German, the child can claim German citizenship only if paternity is proven before the applicant's twenty-third birthday.

Over a quarter of the foreign residents in Germany are Turkish, many of them born in Germany of Turkish parents who were also born in Germany—the grandparents were the workers invited to help rebuild the western side of the country after the war, when there was a labor shortage. Naturalization is an arduous and rare process. Consequently most Turks in Germany are not German citizens, and despite their German birthplaces, their German-language proficiency, and their integration into the economy and society, they are looked at by Germans as foreigners.

Many of the imported workers in eastern Germany were Vietnamese, brought there under contacts negotiated between the Communist governments of East Germany and North Vietnam. Under the terms of an agreement made between Germany and Hanoi after German reunification, most of the forty thousand or so Vietnamese in united Germany were shipped back, often against their will. Hanoi agreed to take them in return for cash offered under the guise of "development aid."

Meanwhile tougher asylum laws—passed to placate the nationalistic right wing and in response to anti-foreigner violence—make it more difficult for refugees to settle in Germany. Nonetheless the government remains adamant about the "Right of Return" law. "The gate remains open," the Foreign Ministry has reiterated in a formal statement on the issue.

Content in the bucolic setting of her new home, Gerta Rothermel sees no moral conflict regarding the preferential treatment she has received. "They are not Germans," she says about the German-born Turks and Vietnamese, while insisting that there can be no question she is German. "Germany is too small," she says, to accommodate the Turks and Vietnamese as citizens. "It is different in America. There," she explains from her European tribal perspective, "there is no nationality. There, there are Americans. He who is born there is at home there, and that is good. That is America. America is advanced."

Into this bizarre immigration mix, Jews move from the former Soviet bloc to make their new homes. With their guaranteed immediate citizenship and social entitlements, they are obvious targets of resentment from other immigrants denied such benefits.

8 □ Along the Border That Jews Can Ignore

AFTER THE WALL was breached in 1989, Chancellor Helmut Kohl pledged prosperity to East Germans. He urged unification promising to spread West Germany's postwar economic miracle to the poor Communist East. His myth ensured his reelection, the agreement to unify, and his place in German history. But the stark reality of vast unemployment, lingering environmental devastation in the East, and the "Wall in the head" mentality that continues to divide the two Germanys, all make it much easier for neo-Nazis to recruit.

The growing German Jewish community has found itself forced to acknowledge a dark undercurrent of prejudice, despite the laws offering Jews sanctuary and equality in Germany. Throughout the 1990s Germany continued to struggle with its need and desire to come to terms with the legacies of its Hitler era as East and West Germany sought to reconcile. The conflicted German national attitude toward outsiders was personified and articulated through this decade by the statement from Kohl that "Germany is no land of immigrants." His barely shrouded subtext was not missed by xenophobes and flagrant German ultranationalists. Nonetheless Berlin's police aggressively protect and defend immigrants and hunt down those who would harm them. Despite that policy and despite the statutory generosity of the federal and local governments, and the welcome offered by many Germans to the Jews seeking sanctuary, the number of anti-Jewish crimes in Germany continues to increase.

HAPPY-GO-LUCKY accordion riffs, recorded on the streets of Slubice, Poland, fill my office as I write. As the accordion plays and I work, I hear again the footsteps on the tape of Germans traveling east for bargains: haircuts a third of the cost in Germany, leather clothing 90 percent cheaper. Vodka and cigarettes at lower prices too. German voices join the street sounds captured on the cassette; taxi doors slam. The accordionist, seeing my microphone, plays vigorously.

On a late winter afternoon I stroll across the Staatsbrücke from Frankfurt an der Oder to Slubice—from Germany into Poland over the Oder River. The sun is breaking through the clouds, glistening on the river. On the Polish bank, fishermen wait for a nibble on their lines. The walk takes me just a couple of minutes, and I share the bridge with a crowd of Poles and Germans crossing back and forth between the two countries.

Taxis line the street where the accordionist sits on a box playing for strong German currency, and I hail one of the cabs for a quick ride to the Poland market. This is a vibrant and bountiful open-air festival of fresh meats and cheeses, fruits and vegetables, tobacco and alcohol, Levis and Polish crafts, ghastly quasi-pornographic paintings swirling in color: the Polish equivalent of Tijuana's velvet Elvis. The hawkers peddle their wares singing out in German; the mostly German customers are seeking bargains. I walk up and down the rows of appealing produce and intriguing handiwork, waving off the offers from the merchants as I look for the merchandise that the German border patrol chief told me I'd find not only here in Slubice but at similar markets on the Polish side up and down the 431-kilometer German-Polish border. Finally I see what I've come looking for: a display of binoculars and single-lens scopes.

"Are these infrared?" I ask the Polish man selling the scopes.

"Yes," he tells me.

"Are they from the Russian army?" I ask.

"Yes," he says again, "Russian army."

As the Russian army left East Germany after German unification, soldiers being paid in nearly worthless rubles and struggling to survive sold military equipment of all types to the highest bidder, including sophisticated equipment such as infrared and starlight glasses. The binoculars I check out are connected to a series of straps so that they can be worn like a helmet and used hands-free. I look through them, and the Polish merchant switches on the power. The market scene in front of me lights up in eerie black and white. Actually, I learn later, the binoculars are not infrared but a Russian version of a starlight scope—a device that amplifies what little light exists at night.

"How much?" I ask him.

He wants about two hundred dollars for the night-vision glass. It is a useful tool for smugglers watching out for German police.

ORTWIN POPP is the Bundesgrenzschutz Polizeidirektor, the federal border patrol chief, for the German-Polish border; he's in charge of the German Border Patrol for the length of the border. We meet in his office in Frankfurt an der Oder, in a reconditioned building that formerly held offices belonging to the East German government. The distinct smells of East German public buildings, smells dominated by harsh government-designed soaps, have been exorcised by German unification.

"We have to control the whole Polish border." Ortwin Popp's English is precise, with a clipped German accent. "I'm responsible for all 431 kilometers. We have to control the border crossing points. I have 28 border crossing points, and we have to control the traffic."

Popp is a roly-poly smiling man, anxious to explain his work. First he talks about his first trip to America, several weeks with his family in a rented car touring the West. His eyes flash his continuing excitement with his world travels as he tells stories about the majesty of the Grand Canyon and the spectacle of the California coast. Polizeidirektor Popp is convinced that securing Germany's eastern border from the hordes of people in the former Communist bloc who wish to migrate west is important work.

"Here in Poland it starts," he says about immigration from Eastern Europe to the West. "But I can tell you that at the Polish-Russian border, when they come in, they see the Garden of Eden." The contrast for most first-time travelers coming west is so overwhelming that still relatively poor and struggling Poland appears as a paradise. "We know that it is not very good over there, but for the Russians who come for the first time over the border it is a real Garden of Eden, yes."

"And then once they get here, to Germany?" I prompt him.

"It's incredible for those people," he says.

Polizeidirektor Popp does not know how many border crossers successfully sneak past his guards and their helicopters, boats, and night-vision equipment, but he does maintain statistics on the human traffic his staff apprehends. About 60 percent come from Romania, another 15 percent from Bulgaria, and many of the rest from the former Soviet republics.

"I must tell you that along the whole border, near all the crossing points, you can find the so-called Poland markets. It is very attractive for the people who are living here on the German side, because it is very cheap over there." Batteries, cassette tapes, bread, and sausages all cost a fraction of their German prices, luring day-trippers from Germany. Red bell peppers, cucumbers, brussel sprouts—expensive crops in Germany—sell at bargain prices. "For the other people who come from Romania and so on, they can get dollars if they sell things they have brought from their home country."

But hard currency is not all that is available for desperate immigrants in the Poland markets and all along the Polish side of the border. "They get a lot of information," says Popp, "about how to cross the border illegally. You can get night-vision glasses from the Soviet army very, very cheap."

And with such glasses, Popp well knows, "You can observe the German border police." His men.

Popp is certain that although many of the immigrants simply seek a better life in the West, too many of them are seduced into a life of crime in Germany. Drugs and weapons are smuggled into Germany with the illegal human trade, be says, and stolen cars move east—the car thieves often simply blast through border checkpoints and past overworked guards, disappearing into Poland and points beyond where an expensive German car can turn a thief into a rich man.

This is how the criminal network operates: The frustrated migrants are contacted in Romania and Bulgaria by professional people smugglers. The system mirrors what occurs on the U.S.-Mexico border, where the people smugglers are called *coyotes*. Along the German border they are referred to as *Schleppers*.

The *Schleppers* use glossy German newspaper advertising supplements to entice their customers. "Look at this stuff," they say as they point to the luxury goods pictured in the advertising. "All this denied you here in Romania and Bulgaria can be yours in Germany."

They offer to smuggle people for no advance fee. They teach people how to enroll in the various social welfare schemes available in Germany. With the changes in Germany's constitution, changes fueled by anti-immigrant fears, it is now a much more difficult proposition even to be considered for asylum than it was throughout the post–World War II years. But if the immigrants manage to qualify for consideration as asylum seekers, they earn lucrative government assistance. Then the *Schleppers* come calling for the payoff.

"On those days when they get their money," Polizeidirektor Popp explains the scam, "some people with white collars come and say, 'Give me the money.'" Simple extortion. "Or they say, 'We have your passport or your identity card. You can get it back quicker if you organize to help some of your people crossing the border. You know already how to manage it. We bring you to the border, and you catch the group and bring them to this or that point.'"

It is to pay the *Schleppers'* bills, say the police, that so many immigrants turn to crime. They steal car radios, cars. They become prostitutes, they smuggle alcohol and cigarettes, they act as enforcers for the *Schleppers*, shaking down other immigrants for cash payments.

On a dark and chilly night I join two of Polizeidirektor Popp's patrolmen on their rounds. We pile into a Volkswagen bus and head down to the river. First we park in the shadows near the railroad and Autobahn bridges. The yawning guards pan the shoreline with their infrared binoculars, watching for telltale movement in the reeds. They wait and watch, watch and wait.

"Look! Over there!" one says to the other. All I see is darkness, but the guard thought he detected interruption created by movement. Perhaps he was wrong. We continue to sit. They look. I strain my eyes trying to see what I imagine must be there, what I know from statistics is occurring: an exodus. Chatter over the walkie-talkies punctuates the still night.

"Thirty-two, thirty-two," our car radios crackle out into the dark, "Where is sixty?" The river bed, the roads and bridges of Frankfurt are filled with Polizeidirektor Popp's men.

Seeking action, the driver eases our bus onto one of the dirt trails that parallel the river. We cruise with the lights off as the other guard scours the landscape with the glasses. We stop at the river's edge, at the side of the railroad bridge, and get out of the bus.

"Here at the railroad bridge," says the more talkative border guard, who walks with me along the tracks, "many of them come over on foot or riding the trains."

This bridge is a major crossing point, he tells me, because

smugglers and undocumented immigrants simply run across it and stumble into the marsh along the German side of the river. Then they try to disappear into the streets of Frankfurt Oder. A long train, laden with coal, lumbers toward us from the Polish side. Its headlight sweeps the tracks with momentary light. Our conversation is interrupted by the screech of the wheels where the track bends, by the engine's whistle, by the metal-on-metal clatter of the couplers connecting the coal gondolas.

Armed with a Heckler and Koch P-6 automatic pistol and a powerful flashlight, the guard illuminates the slowly passing train, searching the couplings between the cars for hitchhikers. It is a coal train and, he tells me, people often hide themselves in the cargo—jumping off the train on the German side, black from the coal.

"Twenty-one!"

"Yeah. Drive fast to the Autobahn . . ."

The radio comes alive again. Another patrol team is in pursuit of a suspected smuggler. We race to a crossroads on the other side of the bridge just as the arrest is made. The prisoner is handcuffed and shoved into the VW bus, next to me. He is wet from running around the riverbank, dressed in black running shoes, black pants, and a black sweater. He looks glum and doesn't talk. He carries a Polish passport, and the police are convinced he's a cigarette smuggler. They search fruitlessly in the underbrush for his satchel of cigarettes before we transport him back to a holding cell at headquarters. The border patrol has twenty-four hours either to deport him or turn him over to a criminal court for prosecution.

Polizeidirektor Popp believes that Germany history—the Nazi crimes and the recent East German dictatorship—precludes securing the German-Polish border completely, just as political pressures make it difficult for the United States to exert its military to seal the Mexican border.

"We don't want to install a wall like the German Democratic Republic built." From a political standpoint, Popp says, the European Community cannot be building new walls on its borders while it is eliminating checkpoints that once separated nations within the Community. "Never. That's not the political idea at all, for the European Union to build up new walls and fences and automatic-firing guns. No, no, no, no, no."

Once Poland becomes a full-fledged member of the European Community, these border wars will move one country east, making Poland the Community's gatekeeper on its northeastern flank. Meanwhile the cat-and-mouse game continues along the Oder, an obstacle that incoming Jews can cross with impunity because of their special status.

9 □ *The Lingering Berlin "Wall in the Head"*

"WE ARE MAKING the Wall go away!" several grammar school children yelled to me as they banged with hammers and rocks against the graffiti-covered Wall near Checkpoint Charlie. They danced around the chips of concrete that fell from the barrier, scooped them up from the ground, and offered me a handful. A few days after the Wall was first breached on November 9, 1989, the clacking of hammers, rocks, and pieces of pipe chipping away at the barrier continued to reverberate through the crisp Berlin winter air.

As East and West Berliners worked together just days before to shatter the obsolescent barrier that had divided the city, euphoria was already giving way to uncertainty about the consequences of open borders between what were still two different states. Not far from the Wall, an old friend of mine, the owner of an exclusive West Berlin restaurant, relaxed over a glass of wine before closing as he worried that the opening of the Wall could foster a dangerous resurgence of nationalism.

"Yes, it's good to see the borders open," he said. "But what is this 'I love you' that people are yelling at crowds of East German people?"

In East Berlin the new and very temporary premier of East Germany, Hans Modrow, said the Wall had protected East Germans from such Western plagues as drugs, crime, and AIDS.

It would not come down soon, he said; the border checks and controls would continue. Soon he was as obsolete as the Wall.

For years the Wall was repaired quickly whenever it was vandalized, but after the November 9 all-night dance party atop it, when the East German government suddenly lifted travel restrictions for its citizens, there was no attempt to fix it. Within days there were gaping holes big enough to peer through to the other side. In some places, twisted lengths of reinforcing steel were exposed. The disrepair gave the once all-but-impenetrable Wall a look of vulnerability and forecast its imminent demise.

In weeks most of the physical wall was torn down, gone. One mile-long section along the Mühlenstrasse was preserved and took on the role of a canvas for a group of international artists. Called the East Side Gallery, one of the panels of this captivating group show is a flag. The heart of Israel's flag, the blue Star of David, is superimposed on the red, yellow, and black tricolor of the German flag. Slim lettering over the flag, along the top of the wall, says simply, *Vaterland.*

LATER THAT NOVEMBER in 1989 I drove south to Leipzig. At the Nikolai Church, a headquarters for East Germans who sought to overthrow their dictators, I joined the regular Monday evening service, a packed house that was as much a political meeting as a worship service. From the pulpit, speakers interspersed cries that there was now no turning back from freedom with prayers asking God to forgive their society for killing the Jews. The words were punctuated with rousing hymns. After the service, the crowd moved onto Marx-Engels-Platz where they were joined by a mob, estimated by police at 200,000, one-quarter of the city's population. One after another, speakers took the microphone and denounced Erich Honecker and the old government, demanding free elections. The chant *Freiheit! Freiheit!*—freedom—echoed across the square. The crowd cheered itself, clearly giddy about hearing people saying things in public that just a couple of months before would have landed them in jail.

DESPITE CONTINUING ATTEMPTS, especially since German re-unification, Germans and Germany cannot separate contemporary actions and policies from the legacy of the Third Reich. Germany's foreign minister, Joschka Fischer, made that clear in his comments regarding the debate over Israel's continuing conflict with the Palestinians. "Whenever Israel is discussed in Germany," Fischer pointed out, "the fundamental debate about German identity is never far behind. Can we criticize Israel? The very question raises suspicion."

In the runup to Germany's 2002 general elections, one of the leaders of the Free Democratic party, Jürgen Möllemann, speaking about the Palestinian uprisings against Israeli authority, said if Germany were occupied, "I too would resist, indeed violently, not just in my own country but also the aggressor's." Möllemann was accused by his political opponents of kowtowing to right-wing anti-Semites in an attempt to get votes. But Paul Spiegel, the elected leader of Germany's Jews, said Möllemann's remarks were worse than just electioneering errors. Spiegel charged him with promulgating "a dangerous anti-Semitic tradition, which in the land of the murderers evidently still exists." Möllemann also felt free to attack a loudmouthed Jewish talk show host, Michel Friedmann, saying his "intolerant and spiteful style" helped foment anti-Semitism.

In the wake of the ensuing public outcry against his statements, Möllemann made a tepid televised *mea culpa*. "If I have injured the sensibilities of Jewish people," he told the nation, "then I would like to apologize." But he refused to extend that apology to talk show host Friedmann, a decision that inspired Spiegel to denounce Möllemann's "continued strategy of double talk." His party was devastated by the voters, and he resigned his job as the FPD's vice chairman.

IN THE 1980s, before German reunification, Israel's president at the time, Chaim Herzog, visited Germany and proclaimed,

"West Germany is Israel's best friend in the world after the United States." When Ezer Weizman, then Israeli president, visited the unified Germany in the mid-1990s, he marveled at the growing community of Jews living in the country. "I, for example, cannot understand how 40,000 Jews can live in Germany," he said. "I am unable to understand that, but it is an independent world, so go ahead. The only thing I can say to Jews is what I always say to diaspora Jews. The place of the Jews is in Israel."

Obviously a growing number of German and former Soviet-bloc Jews disagree with Weizman's opinions. In addition, as the conflict between the Palestinians and the Israelis escalated during the second Intifada, a consequential number of Weizman's own countrymen and women applied to Germany for potential sanctuary from the fighting. Applications for German citizenship were filed at Germany's Tel Aviv embassy by more than fifteen hundred Israelis in 2001, and some twice that in 2002. A German diplomat processing the requests called the petitions "insurance," explaining that "the majority of applicants do not intend to move to Germany, they want to stay in Israel if at all possible."

Many Israeli Jews have the same right to come to Germany enjoyed by citizens of the former Soviet bloc. For the Israelis, this right is written into the German Basic Law, Germany's constitution. Any Germans persecuted by the Nazis or who lost their citizenship based on religion, race, or political activity can return to Germany as citizens. So can their offspring and other relatives.

In addition to seeking security from the Middle East conflict, Israelis with German citizenship enjoy the right to seek employment in all European Union member states. After all, a citizen of the new Germany is, by definition, a citizen of the new Europe.

HOURS AFTER the Berlin Wall fell, I booked the next available flight to Germany from San Francisco. The Lufthansa 747 night flight was packed, mostly with celebrating Germans heading home to share the history-making excitement. My seatmate was German-born Ilka Hartmann, a San Francisco–based photographer.

"I was there when the Wall was built," she tells me. She had decided the night before to take time off from work and return to her homeland. "I just felt I was in the wrong part of the world at the moment."

For Hartmann, the end of the Berlin Wall signified the beginning of the end for German guilt. "It seemed like a punishment for German history," she says about the Wall. "It feels like the war is really over for me!" She's smiling, laughing, talking so fast the words spill out in both German and English. "I feel a burden falling off us Germans. I never expected in our lifetime there might be a possibility of the two Germanys coming together. Unbelievable!" She keeps repeating it: "Unbelievable. Unbelievable."

The immediate euphoria generated by the end of the Wall faded fast after unification, replaced with resentment in the old West Germany, where taxpayers still suffer the burdens of rebuilding the devastated East. In the East, frustrations caused by high unemployment continue to fuel xenophobic and anti-Semitic behavior. But in those first days after crowds pushed through the wall from East to West Berlin, Ilka Hartmann's words reflected the feelings of most of the Germans I spoke with.

"I want to see the joy on people's faces, because I saw all those years the sadness. I want to see the difference. I feel like that myself. I feel just like it says on that newspaper headline"— she points to a German newspaper the stewardess is passing out with huge type screaming, 'We are the happiest nation in the world now!'"

Again she talks about the burdens of German history being lifted. "The stress of being a German was that knowledge of our history, of the past, and of the divided Germany and the constant tension and possible danger. It just suddenly fell away.

That is as deep as the joy that the two sides can be together again: that there's hope now for the future, and there's no cold war anymore."

NOWHERE in recent history has a border been more severely drawn than along the Iron Curtain as it ran through Germany, dividing East and West. The restrictive exit-visa policies for East German citizens, the all-but-impenetrable wall, the automatic-firing machine guns triggered by the movement of immigrants making an illegal sprint for the frontier, the watchtowers manned by guards trained and ordered to shoot to kill, the land mines, the attack dogs—all created both an actual barrier and a philosophical statement that epitomized the repugnance of the border.

Not long after the Iron Curtain rose, I returned to what was the East German–West German border at Duderstadt. When the line between the two Germanys was drawn, Duderstadt ended up on the west side. It is a showplace of half-timbered houses, surrounded by a wall of its own—the medieval fortification built for protection. Today traffic is no longer blocked at the border just east of Duderstadt, it's slowed by road work. The old East German border guard station is a field office for the construction company building the amusement park that soon will straddle the old borderline.

An almost full moon lights up the dawn at the *Gasthaus* where I'm staying, just east across what was the border. Teistungen offers none of the glitz that draws tourists to Duderstadt. Instead the old village is still just a couple of stores, quiet streets with little advertising evident, and remarkably inexpensive hotel rooms. Change is coming to eastern Germany, but in most of the region it is coming slowly—and it is still easy to find villages like Teistungen, tucked off the main roads, looking frozen in time, examples left over from years of isolation.

I leave my sleeping quarters for the dining room. Breakfast is included: room and board for about twenty dollars, a fraction of the cost of equivalent accommodations in Duderstadt. The border remains an economic divider. I eat fresh bread, cheese, a boiled egg, and drink coffee as I watch a heavy old woman clean.

"Look out the window," I say, suggesting she take a break from her work and see the dramatic setting moon.

"*Ah, ja,*" she responds—but after a quick look and the appearance of a smile on her worn face, she looks away. "There is too much work," she tells me, and goes back to swabbing the bar.

As she cleans and grunts and groans, we talk about the changes since the Wall fell. Her story is not unusual. She is sad and angry.

"*Die Leute behandlen uns immer als Osten, Osten.*" The people still treat us like Easterners, Easterners.

The soldiers and the barbed wire are gone, she knows, but she insists that the East German–West German border continues to be a real frontier. "They are *Wessies* and we are *Ossies*," she tells me, "and it will always be so. Always."

She acknowledges that the old East German government made mistakes, but she is no fan of the new authority and the laissez-faire capitalism it has brought to her life.

"They say we couldn't travel before," she says with a disgusted tone, wiping down the dark wood of the bar with a wet cloth. "And if you don't have money, you still can't travel." She laments what she sees as the loss of the East German middle class—with so many East Germans forced to seek work elsewhere or languish on employment payments. For her, the fabric of her community has been ripped to shreds. She is disgusted by the spendthrift society she watches on the west side of the border, convinced that the *Wessies* do not know what hard work is all about but simply buy what they want on credit. Although the changes in the economic and political system on the east side have allowed her family to become private entrepreneurs—they own the hotel—she knows that such an opportunity is not only the result of hard work, it is rare. For most East Germans, unification with the West means the end of benefits easy to get used to: the cradle-to-grave guarantee of basic survival: food, clothing, shelter.

EAST GERMANS grew up taught to live without a sense of German obligation and accountability for the horrors of the Holocaust. Theirs was a Communist country, was the official rationalization, and since Communists were victims of the Nazis, East Germans could scarcely be expected to shoulder blame for Nazi crimes. By contrast, their West German counterparts were forced to accommodate an education steeped in the details of what had occurred during the war, taught that Germans must assume and accept responsibility for those crimes. The *Ossies* were taught to blame the "fascists" who ended up on the other side of the Wall, what their government called an "Anti-fascist Protection Rampart," and not to acknowledge any sense of collective responsibility for the Nazi period.

Nonetheless the clumsy East German government was blind to its long list of inconsistencies. A bizarre example of its failure to cleanse itself of its Nazi lineage was the special DDR identity card known as the P.12. This was the card issued to DDR citizens who were considered less than patriotic to the Communist regime, and it announced that the government restricted the rights of those forced to carry it, rights such as travel and employment. The P.12 was known colloquially in East German as a *Judenkarte*, a card for Jews—*Juden* again as a generic and quasi-official term for a member of a despised underclass, this time with no concern for race or religion.

After the Wall fell, the interim post-Communist government in East Germany finally acknowledged that guilt for the Nazi years was not borne exclusively by the West. "The first freely chosen parliament of the DDR admits," the Volkskammer stated in a resolution passed just before reunification, "in the name of the citizens of this country, its share in the responsibility for the humiliation, persecution, and murder of Jewish men, women, and children. We feel sadness and shame and acknowledge this burden of German history. We ask the Jews of the world for forgiveness. We ask the people of Israel to forgive the hypocrisy and hostility of the official policy of the DDR toward the state of Israel."

BERLIN IS A CITY in perpetual crisis, a city searching desperately for its identity. Berliners cling to the notion that their city is a *Weltstadt*, a world city, longingly comparing it favorably to New York, London, Paris, and Rome even while acknowledging that tourists, business, and the world media continue to think of Berlin in the second string of international capital cities.

Before the Berlin Wall finally succumbed, the city offered a perverse cold war lure for visitors: the Wall, seemingly impregnable. Poor Martin Notev swam across the Spree near the Reichstag just a few months before the Wall opened—one of the last of the escapees. He reached the British sector shore but was immediately snatched up by an East German patrol boat and faced a quick trial before he was sentenced to four years in prison and a forty-thousand-mark fine. Martin Notev was a lucky one: the border guards didn't shoot him. Such gritty reality in Berlin drew tourists, diplomats, spies, artists, and a reputation for the city as a unique cold war battleground.

Since its wild heyday in the 1920s as a creative, mercantile, and political crossroads, Berlin suffered first as the oppressive, murderous, criminal headquarters of the Nazis, then as a bombed-out wasteland. It became a bizarre and tense flashpoint of the cold war and finally a focus of hope as the Berlin Wall crumbled.

After German unification, the city began to redefine itself once more. Berlin again hosts the German government as capital city. The Reichstag is rebuilt for the parliament with its glistening glass dome (after the artist Christo wrapped it in an attempt to exorcise its ghastly ghosts). Rents rose, traffic grew worse.

Shortly after the Wall fell, Berlin began calling itself *Baustelle Berlin*, construction-site Berlin. The scar where the Wall split the city rapidly filled with new buildings, but even this flurry of activity added to the angst over identity. The physical memory of the Wall—the barbed wire, the guard towers, the guards and dogs—was erased so quickly that tourists now stumble around Checkpoint Charlie (near where Martin Notev sought his freedom) searching for some idea of what was once there. There are precious few places where pieces of the Wall remain; the terror of soldiers shooting civilians as they crossed from East to West is replaced with lively cafés and souvenir vendors. As all the construction cranes and holes in the city become huge apartment and office complexes, neither the old prewar nor the old pre-Wall Berlin is rebuilt. The enormous city is something new and different, and Berliners struggle for a sense of what that new Berlin means to their own lives.

Despite the disappearance of the Wall, Berlin remains divided. More than a dozen years after the Wall fell, after unification of the city and the two Germanys, there is amazingly little interaction between the two sides of the city. Newspaper circulation is a good indicator. West Berlin newspapers sell few copies on the east side, and those newspapers read by East Berliners enjoy few readers on the west side of the line. The reason is not merely habit. East and West Berliners have different priorities and interests. An *Ossie* reader is more likely to be worried about rising prices, loss of jobs, coping with still-foreign concepts, ideas, and systems imposed by the West. A *Wessie* reader is apt to be looking for entertainment or news from the financial or fashion worlds, where *Wessies* have the luxury to play.

"Are *Ossies* better in bed?" screams the question on *Arabella*, a tabloid-TV talk show popular across Germany. Arabella, who took off her own clothes for *Playboy*, struts back and forth across the set, from audience to guests, building her ratings on the reality that there are still two Germanys—not just politically but perhaps even sexually.

The Berlin journalist Christian Bauschke is specializing on German unification issues for the weekly newspaper *Wochenpost* when we meet. He tells me he believes too much emphasis is placed on the lasting differences between East and West.

"Sometimes it gets quite ridiculous, when they start to say the West German *ja* is short and tough, whereas the East German *ja*"—and he prolongs the vowel—"is smooth and insecure. This is a ridiculous point. This exaggeration of such differences should end."

Bauschke and I eat in a Turkish *Imbiss*, a snack bar, in Kreuzburg. The culinary borders are blurred to distraction in Berlin. One new restaurant on Alexanderplatz offers Mexican tortillas filled with German fried potatoes, scrambled eggs, ham, and a globby processed cheese, and it advertises the concoction as *auténtico* burritos. At the Turkish restaurant we order *börek*, a dough filled with spinach, and wash it down with cappuccino.

"Of course there are differences between the mentalities," Bauschke says about the two Germanys. He cites a sociological study that asked both West Germans and East Germans to consider their identities. "The West Germans described themselves in a way that fit the clichés perfectly. West Germans are cold, they think only about careers, and they are incapable of showing emotional feelings." East Germans also stereotyped themselves. "East Germans are the contrary. They don't know about careers, they are insecure, but they are the softer people. You know, West Germans are tough, but East Germans are soft."

There is, as there so often is, some truth to the stereotypes. "The ideal," suggests Bauschke, "is to combine these two characters and make something of it." Nonetheless, desiring and creating borders is normal, he says. "It's a natural thing to have a certain area and say, 'Okay, this is my area and here I try to get along. Within this field I have my social relations. I have my close friends and I have my not so close friends, and I have people I know by sight.' That may be something that offers a certain sense of security, to know where I am and not have the vast openness of the universe around me without a point of return."

That sense of security was lost for many East Germans when the Wall fell. "For me, someone from the West," Bauschke says, "I can try to understand, but I will never be able to feel what an East German has felt because everything has changed in his life. Everything. Insurance, taxes, money became much more important. Career and job became more important. Everything changed. And with this, the idea that his whole life was sort of useless."

Many *Ossies* feel so alienated by the loss of the social security system of the old East Germany that they say they would prefer to live in the controlled environment of the pre-1989 German Democratic Republic. Plenty of *Wessies* in Berlin also miss those good old days, when the Wall kept out crime and the hordes of Romanians, Poles, Russians, and other foreigners now clogging Berlin streets—hustling and changing the face of the city.

Some of those citizens less than thrilled with their reunified country find harmless diversions from the past. *Ostalgie* is a growing business. Nostalgia shops sell inferior consumer goods left over from the old Communist days, memories that provide them with some comfort. A handful of bars and nightclubs in the old East Berlin cater to a clientele homesick for the old Communist culture. Decorated with portraits of Lenin and Honecker, they offer some of the second-rate consumer goods left over from East Germany: gritty toothpaste, soap that doesn't lather well, sweet ersatz champagne. A hotel cashing in on the *Ostalgie* trend reconstructs the Byzantine entry requirements for visitors to East Germany as its check-in routine, complete with a doorman dressed up as an East German border guard. Guests change money for reproductions of East German marks, the hotel's official currency. The dining room offers to reproduce what passed for cuisine in East Germany's roadside restaurants. Videotapes of East German TV offer further entertainment. *Ostalgie* aficionados sit around the hotel bar smoking dwindling supplies of harsh East German cigarettes—Juwel, Cabinet, Real.

"They make borders here in our heads." Joachim Gauk speaks slowly and softly at a table where we sit together in his office, deep in a massive hulk of a government building just east of the gash that was the dividing line sundering Berlin. "It is worse than the Wall in Berlin."

Joachim Gauk was a Protestant minister in East Germany and one of the leaders of the New Forum, a political group that did what it could in the restrictive environment of East Germany to change the policies of the government. After the Berlin Wall fell, he was a member of the short-lived parliament that governed East Germany until unification with the West. We meet after he became chief of Der Bundesbeauftrage für die Unterlagen des Staatssicherheitsdienstes der ehemaligen Deutschen Demokratischen Republik, the German government department charged with releasing information contained in the massive files kept by the East German secret police, the Stasi. Gauk speaks passionately about borders.

"I lived under oppression. They gave me borders, and I didn't like those borders. I fought against those borders and the Berlin Wall. I lived near the Baltic Sea, and I was not allowed to have a boat to sail near the beach. The [East German] Marines controlled every small boat. So I have some bad feelings about borders." He speaks English carefully, searching for the correct words to describe feelings he's thought through and lived through. He is handsome in a John F. Kennedy way: the lines of his face cast a distinguished tone, as does the greying hair. He is convinced that his work releasing information in the Stasi files is important work, and that Germany's policy of opening the files is worth whatever trauma results.

But borders, says Gauk, can also be positive. "Borders are necessary for a good life. It's not possible to live without borders. You are a human, a man, and you live with borders. My hand and my head is a border. My culture, my religion is a border. The street near my house is a border. All these are borders that are helpful in accepting a wide-open life."

For Joachim Gauk it is important that West Germans realize that East Germans bring a unique and separate culture to unification, that they cannot be dismissed simply as people who must learn West German ways and discard their own.

"We want freedom," Gauk tells me, "not only in daily life. A population that has lived since 1933 under dictatorship must change its behavior. Because of that it is necessary to have processes of liberation." One example of those processes was Gauk's important work opening the secret police files. Another is the continuing education required to help the long-suppressed masses in the East from slipping back into a mentality of blaming scapegoats for their misfortune. "It's very important to feel and to organize a liberation for your psyche as well as for your behavior."

AN IDENTITY CRISIS is nothing new to Berlin. During the 1960s and 1970s and on into the 1980s, when the city was a geopolitical island occupied by the Allies and the Soviets and cut off from the rest of Germany, it thrived in its own strange way as a mecca for spies, adventurers, and misfits. People remained there because it was their family home. Others were stuck there serving with one of the occupying forces. Young Germans flocked to Berlin to avoid the military draft. Thrillseekers came to experience the cold war, living on the edge. There was an energy and electricity about living where the good guys faced down the bad guys, where intrigue was part of the daily routine and immediate war seemed like a perpetual possibility.

Consequently, isolated Berlin began to develop outside of the confining and often oppressive orbit of parochial German attitudes. Separated from the mother culture, Berlin society became enriched by the British, French, and American presence—

even the Soviet troops added to the international influences on life, as did the Turkish "guest workers" on the west side and the Vietnamese brought to do the dirty work in East Berlin.

Once the Berlin Wall came down, even more foreigners saw opportunities in Berlin as a city where they could take advantage of the strong German economy without being forced to live as unwelcome strangers in a homogeneous land. An avalanche of Eastern Europeans pointed their smoky socialist jalopies toward Berlin, like Okies heading for California during the depression's Dust Bowl, trying to gain admission.

Yet many in Berlin and Germany remain afraid of the continuing onslaught of foreigners. On Berlin talk radio, whenever the debate turns to foreigners or immigration, the cacophony of voices on the telephones is overwhelmingly of the *"Turken raus!"*—Turks out!—variety.

A colleague and I were comparing California and Berlin (few similarities, plenty of differences) and were speaking about languages. "About half of all Californians," I told him, "speak Spanish as a first language." And then I mentioned that about 6 percent of Berliners speak Turkish as a first language.

"They are not Berliners!" he tersely corrected me. "They are Turks!"

Aykut Tavsel is one of those few ethnic Turks in Germany who hold citizenship in both countries.

"I feel a bit German. I was born here. I went to school here, I studied here. My friends are German. But anyhow, I don't know why, I feel Turkish. Maybe it's sympathy with the Turks living here and the problems they have. So I'm in between. I'm not Turkish, and I'm not German. I call myself Eurasian."

Well-traveled and well-educated, Aykut Tavsel expresses frustration with German immigration policies as he lingers over his coffee at a Berlin sidewalk café. "Everyone here knows that the Turks who came in the sixties built up this nation after the war. The Turks were needed. Just imagine the German car industry without the Turks. It won't work. Mercedes can't be that big without the Turks." Naturalization of Turks and other "non-Germans" remains rare. It is an arduous process—and it is still discouraged, both officially and informally.

The economic and artistic potency of postwar Berlin comes in large part from its multicultural, multiracial, multiethnic, multilingual, multireligious population. As Berlin sorts out its identity crisis it must realize that it is a unique, strong, and healthy city-state, saved from the dangerous provinciality of the rest of Germany precisely because it is a melting pot of peoples. Berlin is already a *Weltstadt*—a world-class city—in the best possible sense of the term. It can be a city that reflects what this world has to offer by welcoming and encompassing the peoples of the world.

In this era of renewed European prejudice against non-European immigrants, Berlin—despite and because of its horrific twentieth-century past—can be a model not just for tolerance but for how integration creates strength. In its search for identity, all Berlin needs do is look in the mirror, not back at its history, and see itself as it is today: an often raw and sometimes wild beast, full of productive energy. As such it can grow into its role as a successful capital of Germany.

The exodus of Jews to Germany accelerates Berlin's arrival as a *Weltstadt*. As a result, all of Germany profits.

10 □ *Jews Ponder Assimilation*

MORE THAN a dozen years into the exodus to Berlin, Germany is home to the fastest-growing Jewish community in the world. So many of these new Berliners are Russian Jews that the Berlin neighborhood Charlottenburg is again being referred to as "Charlottengrad," a nickname left over from past periods of Russian immigration. Russian restaurants are a common sight in Berlin. The Russian-language press is flourishing. Russian musicians fill orchestras, nightclubs, and compete with buskers from around the world in Berlin's subway stations. I visited one orchestra during a rehearsal at a Jewish community center, an orchestra usually consisting of nothing but Russian emigrés. As a French horn and an oboe warmed up, and a violinist tuned up, I chatted with another violinist who was filling in for an absent player. He was a German but not a Jew, happy for this opportunity to play with polished musicians, unconcerned about being a Christian in an orchestra made up of Jews, telling me music transcends religious and national barriers.

Of course, not all the Russian activity in Berlin is a story of sophisticated cultural events, flourishing students, successful academics and professionals. "There are Eastern Jewish criminals in Berlin as well," wrote the journalist Joseph Roth in the 1920s. "Pickpockets, bigamists and con artists, counterfeiters, racketeers." It's no surprise to learn that the same is true today. Import throngs of newcomers into Germany, especially from a system as laden with corruption as the Soviet Union, and you'll get some crooks.

Russians living in Berlin recently took over the grand ballroom of the Intercontinental Hotel for a party described in the Russian-language Berlin press as an ostentatious display by the Russian mafia. Mafia is a loose word and doesn't necessarily mean criminal activity. But during the period immediately after the Wall fell, the rules, along with the borders, were blurred. Plenty of enterprising Russians (certainly not all of them Jewish) took advantage of the chaotic circumstances to come to Berlin and set up shop. Many traded in goods back and forth between the Soviet republics and Berlin, across the relatively easy drive through Poland. Others dealt in drugs and women. Some of these enterprises evolved into legal and thriving businesses. One result of this commerce is a class of Berlin-dwelling wealthy Russians, and plenty of them were on display at the Intercontinental party.

Hired actors graced the packed ballroom, dressed to play the tsars in a lionization of the corrupt rulers of Russia's past. Fireworks were set off over the stage to create the flaming image of the tsar's crown. The crowd cheered and toasted with champagne brought by waiters and waitresses costumed to evoke the grandeur of the tsars' court in imperial Russia.

Except for a brief photo opportunity as the guests assembled, the event was closed to the uninvited public and the Berlin press. But the participants wanted to document their experiences, so they hired a Russian filmmaker, Grigori, to shoot the evening's festivities.

ANNA AND GRIGORI, recent arrivals in Berlin from Russia, invited me to meet with them at their new apartment, a typical high-ceiling prewar flat, with tall double doors separating the rooms. Their possessions are still in boxes when I arrive. Grigori is banging nails into the walls, hanging pictures. One is a painting of a child looking at a bird in a bird cage. Another bird, a dove, sits on the child's head. Another is a street scene with a decidedly Eastern European feel: mustard walls along a narrow street under foreboding cloudy skies, a forties gangsterish sedan squeezing down the narrow cobbled lane. Anna pulls a portrait out of the stack and tests it against the living room wall over the couch. Their eight-year-old daughter wanders in to check on things, a darling-looking child with thick brown curly hair framing an angelic face. She seeks out her mother for a kiss.

They stop their housework to talk, and Grigori says it was violent street crime, not prejudice against Jews, that convinced them it was time to leave St. Petersburg. Once in Germany, Grigori says, he finally felt safe about letting his little daughter walk down the street without having to hold her hand all the time. "It wasn't anti-Semitism. I lived forty-five years in Russia with anti-Semitism. After *perestroika* and the minuses of freedom, we feared for our lives. It became very dirty." But Grigori maintains fond memories of a safer and calmer time under the restraints of the Soviet system. "Back then, life in that city was much better. In fact it was one of the most beautiful places, and I lived there for twenty-five years." Once Mikhail Gorbachev began to institute reforms, life just got better and better for him. "The best period was the last five years of *perestroika*. Everything I wanted to do, I was able to do. I was the main editor for Lenfilm. I was making movies, showing them in the West." But as was the case in so many places in the former Soviet bloc, those freedoms combined the bad with the good. "Fear was coming step by step. There were the beginnings of crime and uncertainty. My family insisted that I leave the country and go to Germany. I didn't want to go, and especially not to Germany. But they insisted, and that's why I came here."

Grigori speaks with sad-looking eyes. His hair greying at the temples adds to a severe look as he talks about a migration he felt compelled to take. "My [other] daughter was six years old. I remember it was 1986 when *perestroika* started, when freedom had begun, when we could do everything we wanted to do. I don't remember letting my little girl go far from me. I was with her all the time, holding her hand." But street crime increased and invaded the sanctity of her school. "One of the boys was raped in the elevator, and then they killed a girl. I noticed that bandits would follow me when I was shooting movies, and I was afraid they would steal my camera. I was successful but already growing afraid. All these little things frightened me." The move to Germany was an escape. "The first and the main reason was fear for my daughter."

Anna, Grigori's wife, is a published author specializing in the immigrant experience. While pleased with the safe haven Germany provides for her and her family, she thinks many Russians living in Germany are "sitting on their suitcases." That's a phrase popular in the Russian immigrant community. It means they are ready to leave if things go bad again. "When I visit my friends in Israel and America I encounter Russian Jews who say, 'This is our country.' But the Jews who came to Germany, even after twenty years of great success, do not say that."

She is as serious as Grigori when she tells her story of escape from post-Soviet Russia. Her former husband was an art dealer in St. Petersburg. "During *perestroika* those collectors started getting shot. So we ran away. We could go immediately because we had a permit to go to Germany. We fled the country because of physical danger. People we knew, the family of our close friends who were collectors, were shot to death and their paintings stolen. It was a nasty story." She has an austere look as she talks, a look compounded by her short brushed-back hair, high-necked dark brown sweater, and slowness to smile.

Once in Germany she became acutely aware of the divisions in the Jewish community between the German Jews, the Jews from the Soviet Union who managed to emigrate before *perestroika*, and those—like herself and Grigori—who came after the Wall fell and migration was possible without much complication or peril. "When I came here, I wrote a book about this. Of course there is a difference among these Jews. I gave readings of this book in many Jewish communities in Germany. Unfortunately the Russian Jewish community is separate from the German Jewish community. There are always disputes between them. I told them that it's time to come to an agreement because our common grandchildren are waiting for us." Anna says she feels the Russian Jewish community suffers from a failure to consider Germany a new home. "I was very sad when I met the old Jewish immigrants. What bothered me when I met them was that even though they were so successful, almost all of them had an apartment in Israel or America. It's like a safe landing place just in case something happens. They were always ready to leave."

Anna is still trying to determine if she is also sitting on her suitcase. "My readers believe that I know more about this because I wrote a book. When I read [at public readings] from my book, people ask me about my own concerns for the future of our Jewish children in Germany. I wonder myself, because I'm the mother of two Jewish kids. Could they develop the same way as my aunt's kids in Israel or my sister's kids in Boston? It's a rather painful question for me. Would they be able to show their abilities? Would they be able to achieve good positions based on their knowledge and skills and education?"

She pulls out a copy of her book—*My Emigration*—and reads to me her observations on these questions.

We're all different and very tired, those who dreamed or those who refused to go. We always dream of a better future, moved by greed or friends. We still refuse to move on to a better country, to start a new life, not knowing if we shall stay here. We have moved to Germany at the threshold of the new millennium. Will a new wind blow us away? Will it blow us out of the boat? Although our children and grandchildren will be born here, only the grandchildren of our grandchildren can give an answer. There's no prophet in our own country, and what can you say about a prophet in another country?

Anna puts down her book and Grigori joins her on the couch, sitting close. I ask them to try to forecast their own future in Germany, the future for their precious daughter. "When my daughter was in St. Petersburg, I wouldn't let go of her hand," Grigori answers. "As soon as we arrived here, we felt free, and I released her hand. She feels free." The little girl hears us talking about her and wanders to the living room doorway, smiling shyly with a hand covering her mouth. Her father pulls her onto his lap as my Russian translator continues. "This is real freedom. This is home for her. Not because there are twenty-eight different types of cake or a lot of different clothes, or a lot of different toys. She's just free. That's for her. My fear, the fear of a father, doesn't affect her. As for me, the Jewish father, it hurts me that she lives here. I don't want her to become German.

"When I came to Germany with my family, I wanted to leave, but I didn't. Somehow, to make an excuse for myself, I wrote a little script, 'Farewell Germany.' It's a story about us, about our life here. And I wrote, 'Why do we live here? And why doesn't our conscience torture us?' I wanted to say that we can't live here. But it was just hysteria that I splashed onto paper."

Anna recalls that when she first arrived in Germany and introduced herself to German Jews as a writer, she was cautioned about expressing her opinions in Russian. "They said, first learn the German language properly and take an active role in local politics and make a contribution to the culture and try to do something for Germany, and then present your claims. I said, 'Who said that you can write and talk about Jewish topics only in German?'"

So who are you, I ask Anna—a Jew, a Russian, a woman without a country?

"I feel myself a Russian Jew who came from St. Petersburg.

There is such a category. And when I meet my friends, also from St. Petersburg, in Israel and America, we speak the same language. We have a common understanding. Of course I feel myself a Jew. My family members were secular Jews. My grandfather used to tell me, marry someone with whom you fall in love, but please fall in love with someone who is Jewish."

11 □ *Jews Rooted in Berlin*

THROUGHOUT THE NINETIES, the Jewish community in Berlin grew, prospered, and even allowed itself some feeling of complacency in the relatively safe environs of Berlin. As tens of thousands of persecuted Eastern European Jews escaped to Germany, their huge numbers overwhelmed officials of the German government and those of the German Jewish community. But as the decade ended, the elected leader of the Berlin Jewish community, Andreas Nachama, felt satisfied, pleased with the influx of Jews from Eastern Europe.

"I think the most important influence for the Jewish community is that these people are coming," Nachama says. Despite the challenges and problems associated with this unexpected immigration, he sees it as saving the German Jewish community. "What we expected—that the Jewish population in Germany would decline and that it would be a tiny community—has not become reality. The Jewish community in Berlin and the Jewish communities all over Germany are growing." Nachama smiles and tells a favorite story about this happy development. "The rabbi at my bar mitzvah, when I was thirteen years old in 1964, in his sermon said that in the year 2000 I would be one of eight hundred Jews in Berlin. That was the expectation at the time. Today we have almost twelve thousand members here in our community, half of them Russian-speaking Jews. So this is something. History turns around, and you can't predict it."

When the Nazis spread their terror across Europe, one of the families they grabbed in Greece was the Nachamas, shipped—as were so many Greeks—to concentration camps in Poland. Estrongo Nachama survived Auschwitz and then the forced march from the Sachsenhausen camp on the outskirts of Berlin, as the Nazis fled with their prisoners from approaching Allied troops. He settled in Berlin after the war. In 1947 he became cantor at the Pestalozzistrasse synagogue in Charlottenburg and quickly gained fame for his soaring voice. He married a German Jew; Andreas Nachama is their son.

The extraordinary increase in the number of Jews living in Berlin and Germany after the Wall fell initially caused special problems for the existing community of Jews, problems exacerbated by the unexpected nature of the population boom. "I think the most troubling situation was in 1990–1991," says Nachama, "when a large number of Russian-speaking Jews arrived here in Berlin and, of course, the Jewish community was not prepared for it. The new immigrant population almost doubled within two or three years. It was chaotic. Today it's much easier. We have some two hundred new arrivals per year coming to Berlin, and we have an administration that is working with that. We have social workers, we have integration programs. All this had to be created at that time, in 1990–1991, out of nothing. That was a very challenging situation. I would have wished in a way that these people would have come over a longer period of time. But as they came, we tried. Even though not everything was as perfect or as good as it is today, I think we managed the situation."

When we talked, Germany was again in the throes of a national debate over so-called *Leitkultur*, the concept that Germany ought to be populated with citizens who share a common culture, what was being termed a "defining" culture. *Leitkultur* takes on a whole spectrum of meanings in Germany. Some discard it with disgust, insisting it has no place in today's multicultural society. Others—such as followers of the ultraright National Democratic party, the NPD—cling to it as a definition of Germany and what it means to be German: language, common history, cuisine, fashion.

Andreas Nachama considers *Leitkultur* in the context of the influx of Jews from Eastern Europe, many of whom don't speak German, let alone share other typical German traditions. "Defining culture, defining culture," he mulls over the concept. "Every country has a defining culture, even if the defining culture, as in the United States, is the Melting Pot idea. So it's not the term *Leitkultur* that is problematic. It's what comes with it, which means what these people who invented the term think it should be." His worry is that anti-Semites and Germans who want foreigners out of the country will incite violent neo-Nazis and skinheads with a false and insular sense of what it means to be German.

"What should the defining culture be? The constitution? No question. The basic elements of the constitution that everyone is free, that man and woman are equal? No question about that. Even German as the language of this country is no question. But once you start defining things like that in Germany, you get a system, you know?" Nachama understands this element of German culture well, the stereotypical trends toward order. *Vertrauen ist gut*, begins an old German saying, *aber Kontrol ist besser*. Trust is good, but control is better. "So everything will be checked, for example whether your German is good enough to become a citizen or not, to be allowed to be a permanent resident or not. This is ridiculous. This is not culture, this is something like tyranny. So we see this [*Leitkultur* campaign] with a laugh in one eye and tears in the other."

But Andreas Nachama is not greatly concerned with the *Leitkultur* movement. Especially for Berlin, he feels confident that in the years since 1945 Germans have developed a more sophisticated social consciousness. "I think Berlin is an international city, as our governing mayor always puts it. It is a city where you have different cultures, different religions, different ways of life." The values of this multicultural lifestyle are much stronger than the calls for *lederhosen* and cuckoo clocks. "I think," he says with a touch of ridicule, "no one is unwilling to give this up except maybe some people who live beyond the mountains, in little Bavarian villages." He likens the changing German society to a theatre with different acts in progress. He recognizes the specific role he plays. "We as a Jewish community are a minority. A minority is not the majority."

Andreas Nachama

But not all the Jews pouring into Germany are lucky enough to land in cosmopolitan Berlin. How do resettled Jews fit into those little Bavarian villages or the Black Forest? Is there room for Jews in these isolated spots, or should Jewish immigrants come only to places like Berlin, where there's a broader variety of people and a tradition of tolerance?

"Difficult to judge," Nachama acknowledges. "I have never lived in such a small village." Here he makes a point on which most Berliners would likely agree, including Jews, Vietnamese, Turks, and Germans whose families go back to their equivalent of the *Mayflower*. "Even without being Jewish, I cannot imagine—as an urban person, someone who has been brought up in a metropolis like Berlin—living in one of those little villages. Even when I go on vacation, after four or five days I have difficulty staying there because I need cinemas and theatres and coffee shops and all that. If there's just one coffee shop, you know, I get fed up with it after three days. So I cannot imagine how Jews coming from a Russian or a Ukrainian metropolis would suddenly live in such small places and be happy. On the other hand," he chuckles, "that's a way of integration into Germany." All sixteen federal states are receiving Jewish and other immigrants. Both the immigrants and the locals in provincial towns struggle with the changes caused by the new Jewish arrivals. "Let's see what comes out of it. I don't think in the long run Jews will stay by themselves without a surrounding Jewish community in these little places, because they are much more used to urban life."

One thing Andreas Nachama does not question is the strength of the Jewish community in today's Germany. "Five decades after liberation, Jewish communities here have been established, are flourishing, are growing." But he is ever mindful of the challenges and the responsibilities. "Nobody knows what the future will bring. I mean we are in Europe. We know that there's a connection between blood and soil in Europe. If there is a country or people that has learned lessons from Auschwitz, it's the Germans. So maybe there is a future. But I would never be a hundred percent certain, because that's what we've learned from history, we as Jews, that each country can lose its qualities of being civilized. So take every day as it is. Look at what you see and decide every day anew whether there is a future for the next"—he is remarkably conservative about his expectations— "let's say two or three, four, five years or so."

He is similarly realistic about danger. Is Germany a particularly dangerous country for Jews? "I don't think so, but it's difficult to know. You can be attacked on a public train or in a subway or a bus," but he quickly adds, "as anyone can be attacked. Each day is a new thing. But in the last five decades Jews have lived more or less without major problems." He corrects himself and puts his assessment into a European context: "Or let's say that in Germany they have had no more problems than they would have had in France or in England or in any other European country." One of the oddities Nachama points out is the overt anti-Semitism that's expressed in a country with a dearth of Jewish targets. "I think until now most of the neo-

Nazi incidents have occurred at places where there are no Jews. So you have here [in Germany] anti-Semitism without Jews, as in Poland." Certainly there have been attacks where Jews were not present: demonstrations, as in Greifswald, and desecrations of cemeteries. "That's a very typical situation in Europe."

But he insists the statistics do not cause him angst. "I don't think you have many more than eight thousand people all over Germany who are ready to commit right-wing crimes. I don't speak about those people marching in the streets and shouting for the NPD. I speak about those people who are ready to attack someone. Bad enough eight thousand people, but compared to eighty million inhabitants of this country, you have to take it as a relative figure. I don't think you have a smaller percentage of people hating Jews and being ready to commit crimes and to attack people in the United States or anywhere else."

Nonetheless, Nachama is on guard. "There is no guarantee that Jewish life will go on here, that it will flourish, that in ten years' time we will sit here and find that the numbers have doubled. We don't know what the future brings. Prophecy has died out in Israel, and false prophets are stoned, so I won't dare. But we should look very carefully every day, as I said before, at the news, at the situation. These neo-Nazis have already lost their civilized standards. So it's a question of how the majority will deal with it."

Andreas Nachama is relaxed as he reflects. He smiles. "Democracy is something like love. You have to earn it every day. If you have a partner you have to try every day to find a life together. It's the same with democracy. It's not assured with the constitution. You have to bring life into the constitution and life into the constitutional life of the whole country, of the whole state, every day. Even the battle of the vast majority with this neo-Nazi minority is something that in the end either strengthens democracy or we lose it. It's the same thing with love. Either the difficulties you have in your daily life will strengthen your relationship or destroy it."

How to earn that democracy? What to do every day to nurture it? "This is very difficult to say and to urge what should be done," Nachama says, "but I think, as we saw here on November 9, street rallies with large numbers of people show, on the one hand, how few neo-Nazis there are. Strength is shown on the other hand. Those who were at the march and even those who didn't participate but who sympathized with it are the majority. So you can walk upright." Meanwhile he feels strongly about the role of government. "The government should use the constitution against its enemies, that's why we have it. If a party in Germany can be banned, if the government authorities who are responsible for public life find that a party or group can be banned, then it is German law that it must be banned. There is no further discussion. If you find someone who's so far outside of constitutional life that he can be banned, he must be banned." Nachama is talking about the NPD.

Of course Nachama is well aware of the conflicts within the Jewish community in Germany regarding the new arrivals from the Soviet bloc. Critics of the exodus suggest that many of the immigrants are not "real Jews" but are opportunists who have moved to Germany only for economic reasons, because it is such an easy place for someone who can be identified as a Jew to settle. "People from the Soviet Union find Germany attractive, and there are certainly different reasons for that." But he refuses to label the newcomers simply as opportunists. "I think the first reason they leave their home, their country, their language is not economic. It is because Jews are treated badly in the states of the former Soviet Union. If economic reasons also coincide with that, it's good, because they have to survive here. If someone comes here without economic ambition, just to get social assistance, he has no future. Same thing in the United States. People go to America because they want to start a new life, including their economic intentions, so there's nothing bad about that."

Nachama says the United States analogy is apparent in the cultural life that newly arrived Jews add to Berlin. "Imagine

New York, 1939. The German Jews began their influence on the American Jewish scene really in the late fifties. In the first years, economic survival was the first point on the agenda of these people. Why should it be different here? Let's give them another ten years and I'm certain that the influence of the Russian-speaking Jews will be much more visible in our Jewish community here."

If Andreas Nachama, with the understanding he has of the insecurities facing Jews in Germany, received an e-mail or a letter or a phone call from a colleague who had been living in Moscow asking, "I'm thinking of emigrating to Germany, is it a good idea? Is it safe for my family and me? What's your advice?" what would Nachama say?

"I think everyone has to decide for himself. I would tell him that there is a basic anti-Semitism, that there are neo-Nazis on the scene. And I would tell him that something like probably 95 to 98 percent of the population would welcome him. And that, as in any other country in the world, probably also in the United States, new immigrants have to fight. There are no boiled chickens flying into his mouth, that's for sure."

12 □ *Christian Germans Protest Anti-Semitism*

THE CONFLUENCE of German historical events attached to November 9 is noteworthy. *Kristallnacht* and the fall of the Berlin Wall occurred on this date. The Kaiser stepped down on November 9 after Germany was defeated in World War I. Hitler made his first grab for power in Munich with his failed coup on November 9, 1923. That's why November 9 was chosen in the year 2000 for a massive demonstration. A voluntary army of some 200,000 Germans, the overwhelming majority of them Christian, joined to show their rejection of neo-Nazi violence. The crowd was motivated in part by shocking statistics: reported neo-Nazi violence had increased by 50 percent the preceding year. The demonstration was organized by the government, Jewish community leaders, schools, and a coalition of grassroots organizations.

It wasn't the first time post-Wall Germany had attempted to convince itself and the world that the united Germany need not be feared as a breeding ground of hate and violence. In November 1992, as the first surge of startling post-Wall neo-Nazi violence in Germany hit the headlines, the Helmut Kohl government agreed to participate in a similarly motivated Berlin demonstration. That event quickly deteriorated into a counterproductive display as President Richard von Weizsäcker's speech was disrupted by heckling and hurled eggs, tomatoes, and paint bombs.

It is a clear and chilly evening November 9, 2000, when demonstrators begin assembling on Oranienburgerstrasse for the march to the Brandenburg Gate. My pin from that night hangs on the bulletin board in my office: stylized stick figures, the date, and the legend *Wir stehen auf für Menschlichkeit und Toleranz,* We're standing up for humanity and tolerance. Tolerance seems a limited goal for a modern German worried about a resurgence of marauding racial and religious hatemongers. Although it suggests both recognizing and respecting the opinions, beliefs, and practices of others, it carries a condescending potential. "To merely tolerate is to insult," wrote Goethe. He made it clear that a further step is needed by adding, "True liberalism means acceptance."

As the crowd builds I chat with a woman standing in front of one of the army-green German armored personnel carriers, marked "Polizei" with stark white lettering, that is permanently stationed for symbolic and actual protection in front of the New Synagogue. Sybil Uken is wearing her *Wir stehen auf* pin, and she is frustrated, worried that during the 1990s the neo-Nazi movement was allowed to grow without important opposition from the rest of German society. "I believe if popular politicians, especially in the East, had taken this topic more seriously, it could have changed things. I don't believe much in changing by words, but walk what you talk."

Labor lawyer Sybil Uken tells me that the street power of the right wing is not simply a theoretical question for her. Just the year before she was driving on the Autobahn when traffic came to a standstill because a group of skinheads was attacking another group of travelers. She tried to separate the victims from the skinheads with her car. "It was incredible. It was embarrassing. I never thought that in Germany things like this could happen again." Perhaps it was an isolated incident, I suggest, the kind of thing that could happen elsewhere in Europe? "It's true that we are eighty million and they are just a little group, but there are too many who just don't stand up. If people would stand up, these things couldn't happen. There are too many people who think what they're doing is okay. Grandfathers still talking about the Second World War, how good Stalingrad was, and all these things. If people don't stand up and say no, of course these things happen." She's protected against the cold with a bright red scarf tucked into the turned-up collar of her black leather jacket. Sybil Uken is a '68er, an *Acht-und-sechziger*, as the Germans call those who were student activists in the sixties. "In the early twenties they were a little group," she says of the Nazis. "Everybody thought Hitler was an idiot, there was something wrong with his mind. And we know what happened." She shakes her head and raises her eyebrows.

A helicopter flies overhead, police car lights flash, and Sybil Uken ends our chat with optimism as she joins the march. "I think that 95 percent of the German population of eighty million stands up for democracy and stands up for human rights and for tolerance toward other people. It's a minority," she says of the right-wing radicals, "but it consumes a lot of time and energy right now because politics and society and every individual have answered too late to their actions." Responses such as the march are of critical importance, she says. "You have to send a signal." And with that she returns to her work selling *Wir stehen auf für Menschlichkeit und Toleranz* pins on behalf of her political party, the Social Democrats.

THE CROWD gathers slowly and stands around as the street fills. Voices are hushed. An organ-grinder cranks and, in the role of singing political pamphleteer, belts out a song written for the occasion about German so-called *Leitkultur*. Debate is continuing about what—if anything—constitutes a broad-based German culture. Right-wingers want to use *Leitkultur* as a test for citizenship in Germany, or even residency, suggesting that an understanding, if not an embracement, of German *Leitkultur* ought to be required of immigrants. In a satin top hat and tuxedo, the organ-grinder fills the street with words about "Uncle Adolf" and the cuckoo clocks and the war he sent to the Germans as examples of German *Leitkultur*.

Workers fill green balloons and hand them out to passersby, balloons adorned with the words *Nein zu Neonazis*, No to Neo-Nazis. A couple carries a banner reading *Deutsche Leitkultur: Brutal und Stur?* And the "s" for the word *Stur*—stubborn—is written as the double "s" trademark of the Nazis. Another banner reads *Meine Leitkulturen* over a row of international flags. Broadcasters are on the air, filling radios and televisions across Germany with live reports from the scene. A marcher holds a photograph taken in 1935 of a sign posted at the entrance to a German village that reads, "Jews enter this village at their own risk." Over the photograph is scrawled *Deutsche Leitkultur*, followed by the words, "NOT AGAIN." A placard reads *Weg mit der NPD*, Away with the NPD, the National Democratic party. Cards are held in the air announcing *Nazis Raus*. A flag displays the international red slash meaning "no" superimposed over a swastika. Marchers from other parts of the city begin to converge on the starting point at the New Synagogue, marchers distinguished by their variety: old and young, blue jeans and suits, beards and clean-shaven, spiked hair and berets. Schoolgirls with a pot of glue and a paint brush stick notices on lampposts.

In a neighborhood where many buildings are still pockmarked from World War II machine-gun bullets, police are out to protect marchers in this demonstration organized by the government, trade unions, schools, and churches. A woman old enough to remember those wartime machine gunners walks down the cobblestones wearing a sandwich board that says both "Peace" and *Frieden* and is decorated with a peace symbol. A man too young to personally remember *Kristallnacht* has a sign hanging from his neck reading "Remember 9 Nov. 1938."

The march starts, and the marchers become louder, some talking, others chanting. Whistles blow, bells ring. But the dominant sound along the route is a group murmur and footsteps.

Marching with his infant son is Berliner Andrew Roth, originally from California. "I'm here because I met a German woman in New York and followed her to Berlin."

"That's me!" says his wife Annie, smiling. "I fell in love with him in New York and we moved to Berlin."

"I have mixed feelings about it," says Andrew regarding the half-dozen years he's been living in his new hometown. "Berlin is definitely the most interesting and the most varied city in Germany. I don't think I could live anywhere else. On the other hand, there are a lot of ghosts of the past that are sometimes interesting and sometimes troubling." He pauses, his eyes wide behind John Lennon glasses, prominent on his face because of his close-cropped hair. This Jewish immigrant could pass as a skinhead. He calls the demonstration a critical move. "I think this event is important because there has been a certain acceptance of a level of right-wing violence and right-wing thought. I think it's important to take the momentum away from the right-wing extremists and to make it clear that their behavior is no longer acceptable and that the large majority of the population finds it appalling. It's important that politicians know that appealing to right-wing sentiments is no longer acceptable. It's important to have people out here in a mass to show the right-wing extremists how isolated they are."

Andrew Roth knows well the neighborhood where the marchers assembled, and he knows the issues being raised by the chants, placards, and speeches of the evening. He's the author of a guide book to the new Jewish Berlin. "Since the collapse of the Soviet Union, Jews are coming to Berlin. There have been some problems with integration. On the other hand, they have helped to make the Jewish community here more dynamic. They have more than doubled its size. I think their presence adds a real liveliness to the Jewish community. True, it has strained the resources of the Jewish community here. It has caused some divisiveness between German-speaking Jews and the immigrants.

"I'm not isolated here," Roth says about being Jewish in Germany, just homesick once in a while. "I love New York," he says, "and I miss New York. But this is about as close to New York as you can get in Germany."

Along the Unter den Linden on the east side of the Brandenburg Gate, the crowd is so thick it's just about impossible to move. Some carry candles. The chatter is still subdued. Banners announce schools that sent contingents.

Jammed into the crowd is Ella Lerner, a Jew who moved to Berlin after Germany's defeat and a wartime spent in China. "I think they're getting along very well," she says of the new Jewish arrivals from the former Soviet bloc. "They are mostly very well educated, and they know how to find their way around. They get a lot of assistance from the community and the government. I know quite a few of them." She is an elegant woman, wearing the black leather jacket so common among German matrons, accented with a designer scarf, gold earrings, bright red lipstick, and arched, penciled eyebrows. Ella Lerner has dressed for the demonstration.

"This is what surprises us all and makes us very sad," she says of the continuing right-wing violence in post-Wall Germany. Her surprise and sadness are not just sympathy for what the new immigrants must face—"not only for them but for all of us, everyone who was left over from the good days gone by." She laughs a caustic laugh. "I tell you, as long as the Americans were here there was nothing of this kind going on. But after reunification, things have changed."

Comments and explanations come readily from the marchers.

"I'm not Jewish," says a law student, "but I saw two Turkish guys some weeks ago get beaten up in front of my window." He looks downcast. "I'm really sick of seeing that. I need to be here to show that we, the Germans, are not Nazis."

Another law student agrees with his colleague. "I'm here because I don't want other people to be threatened with death, like it has been for a time now in Germany. So I'm here to protest

110

against the violence." He says current troubles should not be equated to the Nazi times. "I'm born in 1979, so I don't have a lot of connections to the Third Reich. My grandfathers went to Russia, both. Probably killed a lot of people, I don't know. But then my father was born in '44. He built up a state of democracy, freedom, and liberty. That's why we're here today, to make sure it stays that way. I think the important thing is that we protest against the violence today. The violence in the thirties and forties, that's a long time ago. I think we have a democratic and free state where everyone can live freely. I don't think this is about the Third Reich but about violence today."

Down the street from the law students, restraining her yelping dog, is another young Berliner, high school student Helen Loucos. Sporting three lip rings and a stud through her face under her lower lip, a nose ring and a dart through its septum, at least four earrings, and a haircut that jumps between buzz and blowing in the wind, she says, "I think it's cool that so many people are here. I'm happy that there are actually people in Berlin who show that they think this way." But Helen knows firsthand about prejudice in her hometown, prejudice she imagines the new Jewish immigrants also experience. "I think it's pretty hard for them because there's still a lot of people who think the way the Nazis did, that the Jews are bad. I think it's hard for them, hard for all foreigners, because there are places in Berlin where foreigners can't go because they think they'll get beat up by Nazis."

"Are they right?" I ask.

"Yeah," says Helen, "there are places in Berlin where it's really dangerous for foreigners and punks to go."

Faces are serious as the crowd moves toward the rally at the Brandenburg Gate, where the Berlin Philharmonic celebrates the event with Beethoven's Fifth Symphony under the baton of Daniel Barenboim, the orchestra's resident conductor, a Jew from Israel.

On a huge television screen, the remarks made by German

President Rau are simulcast for the majority of the demonstrators who cannot get close to his podium. "We're working for a Germany in which no one has to be afraid," he says, "regardless how he looks, regardless where he comes from, regardless what he believes, regardless how strong or weak he is."

Paul Spiegel, the elected leader of the entire German Jewish community, quotes the German constitution. "Article 1 of the constitution says, 'The dignity of man is inviolable. To respect and protect it is the duty of the State.'"

A few days after the march, Spiegel and I sit down in his Berlin offices to talk about the increasing number of anti-Semitic incidents plaguing the new Germany.

"Since last year we have had to be concerned about things we thought wouldn't happen again in Germany." He speaks slowly, looking uncomfortable, not just because of the serious subject and his tight three-piece suit and tie, but because he is suffering, along with much of Germany, from an incipient flu, a case of the nasty German winter *Grippe*. "For example, we saw not only that skinheads harassed foreigners, we felt an anti-Semitism. This is a new experience," he says about the level of post-Wall anti-Semitism. He worries that it comes not only from the young and disenfranchised but from what he calls the higher levels of society—older doctors and lawyers and other professionals. "Not activities," he says, "words. We feel it, for example, in conversation. Sometimes I lecture, and afterward I offer to answer questions. And I get questions that are not questions. They say, 'You, Spiegel, because you are on TV every day, you create anti-Semitism in Germany. You Jews are only interested in taking money from Germany.' It's happened more and more in recent months," he says, "not only against Jews. Against Negroes, against other minorities."

I ask him to what he attributes this growing problem. "I think something is wrong in recent years, for example in the schools. I don't wonder that older people have this attitude." He waves his hand in dismissal. "You can't change it, especially if people are more than fifty or sixty years old. But why are younger people anti-Semitic?" He answers himself: "The reason is that they get it from their parents, at home. But what have the schools done about this?" Again he answers, "They haven't done enough, and they haven't gone about it the right way. We have to find a way to talk about the Holocaust that makes young people feel not guilty but responsible. Not for the past, but for the future. For their own future, not only for the Jewish future. We have discussions," he says about his ongoing work developing curricula with teachers and his interaction in the classrooms. "I go nearly every week to the schools and discuss it with young people."

But Paul Spiegel rejects any suggestion that his high profile contributes to Germany's problems. "I think," he starts, and then corrects himself, "no, I am sure that most of the people in Germany do not want what is going on here. They don't want anti-Semitism and they don't want right-wing extremism and racism. But we don't feel they are strong against these things. For example, in the 1970s, when there was left terrorism, you smelled everywhere a total opposition to this terror." He's talking about the harsh police suppression of the Bader-Meinhof gang and other violent left-wing activists who disrupted Germany in the late sixties and seventies. "This you don't find now in confronting this problem."

The German Jewish community, Spiegel readily admits, faces further problems because of its rapid growth. "Don't forget, since 1990, we've got seventy thousand new members in the community. We were not prepared. This is a very big opportunity for the Jewish community in Germany. We are now the third largest in Western Europe! Who would have believed it? When we came back in 1945, we thought Judaism in Germany was finished. There would be no Jewish communities. Now we have eighty-three, with nearly ninety thousand people. We are in reconstruction, new construction. But I think in a couple of years we will handle it."

He listens as I ask a common question: Can there be a normal life for a Jew in Germany? "Yes, but we have a lot of work to do. We need help, not only from the government and not only with money. Teachers, rabbis. This we need. This is our problem." He hopes for continuing help from foreign Jewish communities.

As for the Rojsenblats, the new arrivals from the Ukraine who signed their official immigration papers shortly before I met with Paul Spiegel—papers that stimulated their son to announce, "I will be a German Jew"—what advice does this elected leader of the German Jews offer? Should they get back on the bus and return to Ukraine? "No," he says quietly, shaking his head. "I can't tell anybody what to do or not to do. We never asked Jewish people to come to Germany. We never did. But our feeling is, if Jews decide to come to Germany, it is our Jewish responsibility to help these people integrate here in this country, in this community. And they must have patience. It doesn't work in a day or two. But I'm sure in ten, fifteen years we will have one Jewish congregation." He is not worried about a segregated Jewish community in the future, German Jews versus Eastern European immigrant Jews. "We have the same platform. This is Judaism."

Despite the fact that the German Jews did not ask others to join them, the magnificent growth of the Jewish community in Berlin and Germany seems just and positive. What Hitler and the Nazis tried to kill off is flourishing again. Paul Spiegel agrees that a vibrant Jewish community in Germany is crucial. "I think it is important we came back," he says of German Jews who returned after the war. "We are here. We trust the German people. We trust Germany. We trust German politics. We are here, that's a fact. Now we have to handle this fact." Part of that job is integrating the new, non-German Jews.

Another part of that job is coping with the neo-Nazis. "Yes, there are a couple of thousand anti-Semitic, right-wing skinheads," he cites the lowest estimates. "But don't forget, the German population is 81 million. I get a lot of letters every day. Seventy percent tell me, 'Go ahead. We want Jews in Germany.' Thirty percent say, 'Leave our country. Go somewhere.' Seventy percent!" His voice rises with pleasure. "It's a majority!" His message to them, he says, is not to allow a couple of thousand skinheads to create the image of Germany. "This is not Germany." I suggest to him that perhaps he is underestimating the number of troublemakers. "Okay," he shrugs, "then 10,000. Make it 20,000." He emphasizes that the number is a small percentage of the total population—but it cannot be ignored. The Jewish community must continue to remind the rest of the German society to react to anti-Semitism whenever it reappears.

Nonetheless Germany, he insists, is not dangerous for Jews, and Jews have important work in Germany that goes beyond rebuilding their communities and congregations. "We have to tell non-Jewish Germans that Judaism is not bagels, not Klezmer, not Auschwitz, not Holocaust. We have to tell them what Judaism is about: the relationship between Judaism and Christianity. We have to tell them what Germany lost when they killed German Jewry, what they lost for themselves: in culture, in economics, in science, in everything."

As we say goodbye, I suggest to Paul Spiegel that despite his concerns and warnings, he sounds like an optimist. "I'm an optimist," he agrees with a smile. "Sometimes my optimism is a little bit down, but it comes back again." The smile broadens and he leans back, clearly satisfied with his work.

EXAMPLES OF that emboldened vocal minority in Germany who can't seem to learn the lessons of history are reflected on the letters-to-the-editor pages of the *Allgemeine Jüdische Wochenzeitung*, the national Jewish weekly newspaper, the official paper of the German Jewish community. Judith Hart is the editor. "Years ago," she says, "we had letters, anonymous, without names, without addresses. Today we receive letters with addresses, with exact descriptions of who the people are, what they are doing, what their jobs are, and so on. And they're telling us, 'Leave this country, it's not your country. You're Jewish, go to your country, it's Israel. You don't belong to German society.'" Although she doesn't contact the writers to interview them about their motives, she has her theories. "I think they feel free to voice their opinion. I have the impression that they think it's their right and that no one can tell them not to say it. It's their country, contrary to the Jews, whose country it's not. I think taboo isn't there anymore. At least those people feel that the taboo of anti-Semitism is gone and belongs to the past, not to today and the future."

Does that mean it's dangerous to be a Jew in Germany again? I ask.

She breaks into a big grin at my question and laughs. "Throughout history it has always been dangerous." Serious again, she says, "I'm convinced we're not facing a second Holocaust today, but we really have to take it very, very seriously, because things always start very low key and very 'normal,' and can develop into something more dangerous. If we don't react to these warning signs, something may develop that we don't want."

I ask her to describe the tone of these letters.

"It's really pure anti-Semitism."

She shakes her head with some amazement as she talks about the authors of the letters. "The letters come from all over the country. It's housewives, it's housekeepers. It's elderly people, it's young people. It's a mixture of German society."

Judith Hart prints some of the letters in the *Allgemeine Jüdische Wochenzeitung*, filling a full page of the broadsheet with them in one issue. The idea, she says, "is to show people that this is what people are writing and thinking. Not all Germans, but some of them. Take it seriously. Read it word by word. We don't comment. We just print the letters and the names of the people who wrote them."

The paper continues to run articles and commentary in its

pages about prejudice and about anti-Semitism in particular. "Maybe we can make a difference, maybe not," acknowledges editor Hart, "but as journalists we believe words can make a difference."

RABBI WALTER ROTHSCHILD felt the force of the contemporary hatred of Jews when he was punched black and blue, almost losing his left eye, in a Berlin subway station a couple of months after the November 2000 march. His portrait, complete with bloodied eye and stitches, is all over the front pages of the newspapers as we meet and he tells his story.

Rabbi Walter Rothschild

"There were three lads who had, as far as I was concerned, too much testosterone, not enough common sense. They were being quite aggressive to the driver in a subway train. The driver handled it better than I did. Eventually he just turned around and went away." Rothschild minimizes the crime with his droll humor. He's British.

"As we walked past, up the steps on the platform, I said something like, 'Hey, guys, he's just doing his job.' One of them said, 'Hey, are you Jewish?' I said, 'Of course, naturally.' And, he said, 'I hate all Jews.' I thought that was a little heavy. I mean, *I* only hate some Jews, you know."

He waits for the laugh and gets back to the story. "I thought this was a bit heavy so I said, 'Well, hey, how many do you know?' At which point one of his friends grabbed my hat. I tried to grab it back. I was with a couple of students. One of them tried to grab my hat back. Suddenly out of nowhere comes a fist bamming into my spectacles, my left lens into my eye. There was blood everywhere. They ran off. We ran after them. One of the students who was with me actually caught one. The other two got away. They've all been caught since. I was sat down by one of the subway security guys. They called an ambulance. They called the police."

The rabbi's attackers were not German skinheads but, he says, three young men of Middle Eastern background.

"I wouldn't want to make anyone scared of Berlin. It's a civilized city. I use public transport day and night. My kids travel to and fro on the U-bahn, just go on their own. And we come back late at night from synagogue on the tram and there are no problems, no problems." He was just punched, he's reminded. He acknowledges the attack with a dismissal of its importance, putting it into a context he thinks appropriate. "One black eye in two and a half years."

The rabbi downplays the incident even though it's the second assault on him since he moved to Berlin from England. He says it wasn't part of any anti-Jewish political conspiracy, and he wasn't "stabbed or shot," just punched. "It was an anti-Semitic attack in that respect, but really, it's the first major attack I've had here in two and a half years. Been spat on once, that was all."

It may be no big deal to the rabbi, but official Germany responds quickly to the attack, denouncing it and apologizing.

In his office the Rabbi Rothschild goes through the mail and reads from a letter sent by a Berlin senator: "With great shock and great horror I've heard the news of the brutal attack upon you. In my party we're greatly concerned about the increasing number of attacks on Jewish people and persecutions. We condemn these attacks and think they are most shocking."

13 □ Berliners Analyze the Tolerance Demonstration

MARTIN WIEBEL is a filmmaker. We met by chance during the November 9 march for tolerance. Later we reconnected quite deliberately in a Kreuzburg park along the Spree to talk about his lifelong battle with Germany's history.

"I was born in Berlin in the middle of the war in '43, precisely in the week of the Stalingrad battle," he recounts by way of introduction. His eyes look cheerless as he tells his family story. "My grandparents and my parents were born in Berlin too. So I am of the generation of the sons and daughters of the German soldiers who brought war to Europe and the world." This clearly is not a new conversation for Wiebel. He's been shaped by this history and has spent a career trying to reconcile with his family and national history.

"Maybe this influenced me very much," he says, "especially after the war, growing up in Berlin and West Berlin under an American education. Our way to democracy was prepared and organized by our experiences with our teachers, and by the American policy against the Russians in the same city."

When we talked, Wiebel had just retired from a career making television films. He decided to return to Berlin, to the neighborhood where his grandparents lived, a neighborhood he says was initially developed by his great-grandfather. He took a job as a professor at a Berlin film school. "For me it is really important to come back to my hometown Berlin. The city has changed. I'm really very much interested in what is happening in the city. Is it becoming one of the capitals of the world, or will it be a small town near Russia?" He smiles. A cold winter Berlin breeze blows his white hair; he's wrapped against it in his greatcoat and muffler. A two-toned European siren from a passing emergency vehicle mixes with his sardonic laugh.

Wiebel is one of those Germans who grew up in the postwar period who feels a sense of responsibility for the crimes of his parents' generation. "I think, yes," he says as we talk about it. "Collective guilt was debated in those days in Germany. The whole of the nation has it." He speaks precisely, choosing his words carefully in English, his shock of grey hair and his salt-and-pepper moustache reminders that Wiebel has lived with this historical shadow for many years now as an adult. "As far as I know, my father died as a soldier, and he was never a member of the Nazi party. But he was a soldier in the German Wehrmacht. He died as an occupier in Norway. He had seen me once, and I had never seen him. So I had no chance to talk with him. But I talked with the family about this. This has not been a left-wing family, not a very conservative family, but it was an anti-Nazi family. On the other hand, if you ask them, 'What have you done? Did you resist, and how did you resist?' you find very small, very shy protests. My mother, for example, was a member of the Protestant church. I got my name from one of the Protestants who was in the fight against Hitler, Martin Niemöller. So I'm called Martin Wiebel."

Pastor Martin Niemöller was an anomaly among German Protestants. Although an early supporter of the Nazis' "national revival," unlike most Protestants he actively opposed Nazi racism and Hitler's interference in church affairs. From his Berlin church in the affluent Dahlem neighborhood, he organized his colleagues and parishioners to work against early anti-Jewish actions of the Hitler regime. He refused to answer questions about his personal racial heritage. Hundreds of his congregation supported his actions. He announced to the

120

Führer, "We too, as Christians and churchmen, have a responsibility to the German people which was entrusted by God. Neither you nor anyone else in the world has the power to take it from us." For his resistance, Niemöller was arrested for "abuse of the pulpit" and sent first to Sachsenhausen and then to Dachau. He spent seven years, until the end of the war, in concentration camps.

It was Niemöller who, after the war, spoke so poignantly about his lack of resistance to the Nazis. "First they came for the socialists," he said in what became a famous speech, "and I did not speak out because I was not a socialist. Then they came for the trade unionists, and I did not speak out because I was not a trade unionist. Then they came for the Jews, and I did not speak out because I was not a Jew. Then they came for me, and there was no one left to speak for me."

But Martin Wiebel downplays the importance of the choice his parents made for his namesake. "These are little signs of resistance. But it was not real opposition." His sad eyes are impossible not to notice as he tells the family story. "So maybe I felt, as many of the German bourgeoisie, in a real way guilty for what happened to the Jews."

He recounts typical West German student days: school trips to concentration camps, and much formal analysis of the Nazi era in an attempt to understand why it occurred. That study, along with his observations of the post-Wall resurgence of right-wing radicalism, scares him about the future.

"We are," he says about himself and his contemporaries, "very fearful about what is happening today in our country. Most of the people of my generation participating in the march want to show everyone the world: please believe that the majority in Germany have learned something from their history and don't pay attention to these small activities on the right."

But why, over half a century later, should Martin Wiebel himself feel guilty about the crimes of the Nazi period? It is a question he's thought about for most of those years.

"I think this Nazi period and what happened to six million Jews in Europe is a single special event connected with German policy, with the German people, and with the German nation. I'm part of Germany. I'm personally not guilty. Even my father seems to be not a guilty man. That's different from other children whose fathers or mothers had been very active in the [Nazi] party or the SS. But the nation has something to remember," he points to his head, "for all time. Remembrance is the main thing we can do. This means that we probably have a special need to be very aware and pay attention to what is going on in our country and even in other countries. We have to fight against the idea of bringing back the past, and we have to do it as early as possible."

An example of that type of productive activity for Martin Wiebel is the welcome Germany today offers to Jewish immigrants. "When I grew up after the war, the Jewish community in Berlin was very, very small, I think not more than two or three hundred people. It had no big influence on Berlin policy or on Berlin society. This has changed, as everything has changed in Europe. Our border is open for Jewish people from Russia, from the East, and they are coming and the community is growing." But Wiebel questions whether most Berliners favor this new Jewish immigration. His history-based skepticism leads him to believe that Berlin and Germany feel politically compelled to invite Jews to immigrate while many Germans wish these newcomers would stay away. He worries that anti-Semitic right-wing propaganda and violence indicate that prejudices still exist throughout too much of German society. "Because of history, it is so important to look at every small incident, because it may be a sign of a new tendency. This is one part of the problem that Germany today has with foreign people in general. We are debating in Germany, do we open the door—the boat—for everybody? Not only for the Jewish people coming from the east, people from other countries too. There is a strange debate about this. I think we have to defeat those tendencies in the debate

122

that seek to build a wall around the new German society against everything from elsewhere."

Even as Martin Wiebel ponders the dangers of "a wall around the new German society," he understands and appreciates the basis for the privileges afforded Jews who wish to become Germans.

"Yes, I think so. Because of this historical guilt, the administration treats Jews differently. The political debate in the country is to open it for everyone, not to have extra fences for special groups from special countries. If Germany is an open democracy, then it must be open for everyone. Maybe they can find a system: how much from each country—as the Americans have it."

But for Wiebel, the immigration of Jews is of paramount importance. He believes that the rebuilding of the Jewish community in Germany—and particularly in his hometown Berlin—is critical to his generation's response to the Nazi era.

"I think there is a place for a Jewish community here. I would beg Jewish people from other countries to come to our country and feel free and unafraid. As recognized, the majority in this country are not like their parents or grandparents. Probably it's necessary to build new Jewish communities in this country. On the other hand, it means that Germans must have a very normal relationship with the Jewish communities. One problem of our generation has been called philo-Semitism. A strange reaction of our generation. We have to learn that even this is another wrong way of handling the problem."

Washington Post reporter Marc Fisher encountered philo-Semitism when he lived in Bonn and Berlin from 1989 through 1993. Fisher found it curious to see Germans apologizing when they met Jews and insisting that the postwar generations could not be considered personally guilty for Nazi crimes. "Jewish foreigners who spend time in Germany are often confronted with these confessional moments," he wrote, "and few have the slightest idea how to react. I know I didn't."

"We have to be very normal," Martin Wiebel insists, regarding the relationship of non-Jewish Germans to Jews, "as we have to be to every other religion or nation. Maybe this is what Germany can do. I think around 10 percent of the German society is radical right, just 10 percent. And 90 percent of the nation is different."

Nonetheless, Wiebel isn't overly enthusiastic about the opportunities for a happy life awaiting Jewish immigrants in Germany. He laughs with discomfort, sighs, grunts, and obviously is thinking hard as he stalls with a lingering, "Yes, well," before he answers the next question. "If I got a letter from someone from Eastern Europe—a friend or a colleague—and he asked me: Should I come with my family to Berlin, and what do I have to expect? I would say, Be confident that you can make your living here, probably a little bit better than in Uzbekistan. But it's not easy. It's like in other countries—you have to find work, you have to find some money, you have to find friends. You have to find your community, which is difficult. You will recognize that most people in Germany will be friendly to you and will help you. But to be sure, there are problems in some parts of the country with a minority of the society. What you read in the newspapers is correct. It's not as big a problem as you may think. Make your own life and fight for yourself and look for people with whom you can cooperate."

The hundreds of thousands who turn out in German streets to demonstrate against neo-Nazis are that extended community, according to Wiebel. "The majority will protect you. This is the signal from Berlin to the world. The demonstration speaks to the international public and to Jews all over the world. You can trust Germany. The majority of this country, the majority of the generations are open-minded and tolerant. They will accept you and they will help you and not hurt you. If you read something in the newspapers about the desecration of Jewish graves, about vandalism against a synagogue, something like that, all this is correct, all this happens—but it comes from a small minority.

This is not representative of the country and not what you will find when you come to live here."

The boat is not full, Wiebel is certain, especially regarding Jewish immigration. "We lost the Jewish people. Germany lost the Jewish people. Especially in my field, in film. We lost Jewish humor. There is no humor in German films." He shrugs his shoulders, quickly adding, "There is a special German humor, but it is not very interesting to the world. We lost a lot of talent in the film industry. I would like to have them back, if they want to live here and work with us."

A FRIEND AND COLLEAGUE of mine from the generation after Wiebel's disagrees with the filmmaker's positive interpretation of the street demonstrations. "Rubbish!" Klaus Goldhammer tells me as he looks at my *Wir stehen auf für Menschlichkeit und Toleranz* lapel pin. With his new Ph.D. in media studies from Berlin's Freie Universität hanging on the wall of his office on Oranienburgerstrasse, just a block from the New Synagogue, Goldhammer watched the streets of his neighborhood fill with the crowd and its placards repeating my pin's call for tolerance.

"I don't mind you being enthused and feeling good about it," Goldhammer lectures me after I tell him what a positive experience it had been for me to join those masses in the streets. "But from my point of view there are many, many people walking there who are doing it more for their own peace of mind rather than for anyone else's." His skepticism about the marchers' motives, his cynicism about the march's value, were disarming. "We call these people *Gutmenschen*," he says with dismissal, "people who want to feel that they are doing something good, but with no practical results."

We're standing in front of a graffiti-covered wall at the Friedrichstrasse S- and U-bahn station, enjoying the unusually sunny Berlin winter weather. I suggest that hundreds of thousands marching through the streets is an important statement. The demonstration is headlines in newspapers worldwide.

"Yeah, it's in the newspapers," says Goldhammer, "but it doesn't change anything really. Because the people who are causing the problems—the skinheads, or the right-wings, or whatever—they are not changed or touched by it. It makes no difference. In fact I think it is not helpful to make such official statements." He's referring to the government involvement in the organization of the Berlin march, the president's speech, the Berlin Philharmonic's Beethoven. "Meanwhile the police force in East Germany is still more or less sympathetic to the kind of political or right-wing activities that you see happening. That's a problem, and that doesn't change just because of some people walking down the street." Notice that Goldhammer doesn't use the politically correct terms "new states" or "eastern Germany" when he refers to the old German Democratic Republic. To this *Wessie*, ten years after unification, East Germany is still East Germany.

I argue with him, asking him to consider the impact of 200,000 citizens "walking down the street" in a city of 5 million. Doesn't such a huge protest help change society?

"Don't get me wrong," he says. "Sure I hope it changes the society. But I think it's only one step forward. What we need much more is education and support for those people who don't have much opportunity in Germany and who start all the trouble. That's more necessary than anything else. Also, we had right-wing brutalities for ten years on the street and never, ever was there a serious response to them. We had candlelight vigils all around the city of Berlin trying to make a statement against the right wing, but they didn't change anything. That was 1993, 1994, and since then many people have been killed by the right wing. We've had a headcount of ninety dead by the right wing in Germany, and that doesn't change because of any demonstration."

The next obvious question for an irritated observer such as Klaus Goldhammer: What ought Germans to do about the increasing right-wing violence? He worries that too many politicians are, as he puts it, "playing with firesticks," using language

126

that suggests to the troublemakers some official understanding of their frustrations, if not their illegal actions. That must stop, says Goldhammer, and at the same time "there has to be something done about the future in terms of jobs and work and opportunities for these people who lean toward right-wing extremism. I think there must be a campaign to explain to people what they're doing to their own hometown if they start things like that." He's convinced that the continuing attacks in "East Germany" will limit foreign investment in the struggling region, making problems there worse.

Not that Goldhammer believes there are more such attacks in his German metropolis and its environs than in other European cities. But he is convinced that German history mandates stark and broad action, not just that walk down the street he scorns.

"There is a difference in terms of our history and the guilt that is engraved into German history."

Will there always be this difference? Does the guilt ever get shed?

"I don't know, I don't think so," his eyes look away, squint off into the distance. "If you really want to act sensibly, you should never get rid of it or get over it. But one has to deal with the consequences. Maybe what we see now is a backlash against what we have had for forty years—Germans trying to be cautious toward any kind of right-wing extremism. Like during prohibition, when everyone was trying to get drunk. We had a prohibition on right-wing extremism."

14 □ *Inside an Insidious Neo-Nazi Parade*

ONLY A couple hours' drive on two-lane blacktop country roads from cosmopolitan Berlin, deep in the heart of what was East Germany, is the university town of Greifswald. More than ten years after German unification, the German economic miracle has yet to reach most of the old East, a region where democracy is still an alien concept. I traveled to Greifswald because the neo-Nazi movement, fronted by the still-legal NPD—the National Democratic party—was there to protest the government's effort to ban the party. The party's platform is based on driving foreigners out of Germany.

Almost simultaneous with the beginning of the flow of Jewish immigrants into Germany, and stimulated by the failure of unification to deliver the promised prosperity in the former East Germany, Germany and the world were shocked by the surge of violent neo-Nazism in its midst. The embarrassed government initially tried to deny the problem and then attempted to cover it up. Almost a decade passed before the government was forced to take seriously the threat to German democracy embodied in the small but growing neo-Nazi movement with its skinhead "street soldiers" who, under the right-wing extremist leadership of the Orwellian-named National Democratic party, vow to reclaim "Germany for the Germans!"

These criminals—who point with pride to their lineage with Hitler (while taking care not to violate de-Nazification laws)—

have manifested their hate-filled philosophy by marching to inspire fear, and by torturing and murdering at random. Anyone who appears not to be a stereotypical blond, blue-eyed German, or who does not sound like a native German speaker, is a potential target.

Government officials, desperate not to be perceived as reincarnations of police-state brutes, were stunned by these crimes and offered only the most tepid responses. Their flaccid reaction sent a message to the neo-Nazis that the government didn't really object and would not deploy its considerable resources against the self-anointed heirs to Hitler's creed of hatred and destruction.

Since World War II the German government has banned only one political party because it violated the law designed to prevent neo-Nazis from taking part in the official political process. A direct attempt at reinventing the Nazi party, it was banned in 1952. Only one other party has been banned since the war. In 1956 the government outlawed the German Communist party. Finally, in the late nineties, the government tried again, this time taking action against the NPD. Interior Minister Otto Schily initiated the case against the National Democratic party, telling reporters, "This is a party that generates violence. There is an essential kinship between the Nazis and the NPD." While pursuing the ban, Schily increased police activities against the NPD, explaining, "Forbidding a party is one action against right-wing extremism. But not the only one." Nonetheless the case quickly turned into a soap opera of errors.

In the 1960s Otto Schily had made a professional transition from a business lawyer to a lawyer defending the radical left. One of his clients was a man named Horst Mahler, who was eventually convicted of aggravated robbery and of co-founding the Red Army Faction. Schily tells the absurd story of how that case was lost and Mahler was sentenced to twelve years. "I defended Mahler in the Moabit courthouse, and I gave quite a decent closing argument—at least I thought it was, maybe even a little more than decent. And then I sat down, and the defendant, Horst Mahler, had the final words. And his final words were, 'You don't talk to judges. You shoot at judges.' Well, that was it for me. All I could do was bury my face in my hands. The whole argument had been for nothing."

Fast-forward a generation and the same Horst Mahler is out of prison and has flip-flopped politically from the extreme left to the extreme right, becoming not only a member of the NPD but also its lawyer! Again, in this new job, he foils Schily. The government's initial case against the NPD was based largely on the testimony of an informant: one of the founding members of the party who turned state's evidence. As the case proceeded, it was determined that this crucial witness had been a paid informer, paid by the Interior Ministry for his work against the NPD. This fact all but destroyed his credibility, and along with it the government's case. The payoff predated Schily's term as Interior Minister but nevertheless reflected poorly on his handling of the attempts to outlaw the NPD.

For his part, Schily sees no conflict between his days as a lawyer for the radical left and his work as Germany's chief law enforcement officer, just as he sees no conflict between harsh post–September 11 anti-terror police actions and a free society. "This antagonism between security and freedom does not exist. That's what I keep trying to make people realize. Anyone who is threatened by crime—by murder or battery, by assault or extortion—is not free. And the constitution gives the state the responsibility for protecting the people against crime. You can read it in Article One of the Basic Law."

THE MAYOR of Greifswald tried to prohibit the NPD demonstration, but the courts ruled that because of Germany's law protecting freedom of expression, the march could not be prevented. The marchers assemble at the train station, a few hundred of the neo-Nazis protected by hundreds of riot police. Martial music is playing on loudspeakers. Placards and banners demand that the government not ban the party, one calling for a "free Germany, not a U.S. colony." Marchers hold the NPD flag with its typography and coloring so reminiscent of Nazi graphics. The marchers and police prepare side-by-side. The police pull on their helmets and gloves, adjusting their plastic shields, billy clubs, and knee pads. They're wearing full green jumpsuits. The marchers unfurl their banners and try to line up in some semblance of order. Mostly middle-aged and young men, they too seem to be in uniform: plenty of shaved heads and leather jackets. They begin to march toward downtown, chanting their resistance.

Neo-Nazi in Greifswald

At the same time, just a few blocks away, separated by the police from the NPD demonstrators, thousands of citizens rally against this neo-Nazi march and in favor of diversity and acceptance. Hundreds more local citizens line the route of the march, shouting, holding protest signs, a few hurling eggshells filled with ink at the marchers. "Life is colorful" reads one counterplacard, held by a man squatting behind his son. Hand prints in all sorts of colors decorate his cardboard sign. His toddler is holding another little sign. "No violence," it says. A woman, clearly old enough to remember the thirties and forties, is screaming hysterically at the marchers. *"Nazis raus!"* she yells, "Nazis out!" Her face is deeply lined, her blond hair short under a knit cap, her bright blue eyes indignant as she yells again, *"Nazis raus!"* and then adds, *"Schweiner!"* Pigs. Other townsfolk just look deeply worried as they watch their usually quiet main street.

"I'm seventeen," says one shocked student, shaking her head, watching the parade. "We can't believe it. We don't know what to say. It's unbelievable, stupid, and dangerous," she tells me as another martial song—reminiscent of banned Nazi-era military tunes—plays over the NPD loudspeakers.

"There's no way we can tolerate this," another student, a knit cap pulled tight over his head, tells me. He's out of breath; he's been busy counterdemonstrating. "It's not only a shame for our town but for our nation." He believes the NPD should be banned. "I'm very sad about this," says still another. While we're talking, an egg flies over us toward the marchers, who are chanting, "Free! Not banned!" He looks over at the march. "We really have to take care. We really have to watch these people. It's not easy to handle."

A couple looks on. "How does this make you feel?" I ask.

"Sad," she says. "And unhappy."

"What does this mean for Germany?"

"It's sad," he says, "sad for Germany."

"Should something like this be allowed?"

"It's the law," he says, "unfortunately."

"Unfortunately," she agrees.

"Why unfortunately?"

"It should be prevented," he says, "and that's hard to do when the law protects the NPD's right to demonstrate."

"Is this dangerous for Germany?"

"Yes. Absolutely!" they both say.

"We saw what happened in the forties," she says, "and it looks like that again. It feels like we have been transported fifty, sixty years back. It's simply terrible."

"And what does this mean for foreigners in Germany, for the new Jewish community?" I raise my voice. It's difficult for us to talk, the chanting is so loud.

"I think it could scare them, you know?" he says. But then he leans toward me, intense as he makes his point. "There are also lots of people against it, you know. I mean, this is not Germany. It's definitely the minority. One must keep careful watch. Definitely."

"You say this is not Germany?"

"No. This is not Germany." He glances at the marchers, shakes his head with certainty, then adds with a weary smile, "This is not my Germany."

He looks over again at the marchers, calling them a minority.

"We have to be careful that they don't become the majority."

DOWN THE STREET I encounter another sober and sad Greifswald couple, standing in front of a Communist-era block apartment house, watching the chanting marchers.

"We're certainly against it," she says, shaking her head in disgust, telling me they are heading to the counterdemonstration.

"What does this mean for Germany?" I ask them.

"We look back at ourselves and get scared again that the same thing might happen as in 1933," he says.

The chanting in the background is shrill.

"It's just rotten," she says.

"Is this an unimportant minority or the future of Germany?"

"I wouldn't say it's Germany's future," he says, with more hope than conviction in his voice. "There is enough resistance. We'll show them with a counterdemonstration. But the NPD must be banned so that perhaps they can be stopped."

She agrees, "New laws are coming, and we support that."

"Why is this happening in your city?" I ask.

"That's a good question," she nods and ponders it.

But he knows the answer, "They could be anywhere. It's got nothing to do with Greifswald. They picked a place, just like they picked a street."

And she comes up with a further factor, "It's also because many foreigners come here to the university."

"Should those foreigners be afraid?"

"Yes," she nods again, "I would think so."

The march slows and bunches up at a bridge. One of the counterdemonstrators pushes in close to the neo-Nazis with a camera. The contrast is stark. The neo-Nazis with their shaved heads, stalled in the street. The photographer, moving around, seeking his subjects, wearing a winter cap over his long hair. He moves in close to the faces of the marchers, faces that seem locked together in attempts to look somber and important. One of the skinheads comes toward him and, with a fierce look, pushes him back. I start toward the photographer, to talk, when I'm distracted by a commotion on the bridge. The riot police are arresting one of the counterdemonstrators. His hands are already tied behind his back. He's wearing a sweatshirt, and the officers are dragging him by the shirt's hood to a police wagon. The skinheads look on, and clap.

"What's going on here?" I ask the photographer.

"I think it's obvious," he says, breathing hard. "There's a bunch of frigging, shitting neo-Nazis. They're trying to . . ." His voice trails off. He apologizes and says he's too emotional to talk. He needs a minute to catch his breath. "I'm too involved in this situation."

He tells me he's documenting the march, that he's especially concerned about the role of the police. "They have to protect these fascists. Of course, we're here to demonstrate against these fascists. We're a free country. We would like to have the foreigners here. We'd like to be at peace with them. We would like to do everything to make our country colorful and not be these brown . . ." His voice trails off before he curses again, and he smiles with scorn.

"Does this reflect Germany?" I ask him. "Is this Germany or just a few crazy people?"

"This is a part of the Germany we have to live with. It's not possible to say they don't exist. They are here. But I don't know. Have you been to the marketplace? Have you seen how many thousands of people were there? So I guess this is the minority. I hope so because I am German and I would like to live in Germany as a German with my friends from outside."

"What is the message this sends to foreigners who are moving to Germany?" I ask him. "What is the message to Jews who are returning to Germany?"

"Their message, as they sang just a few minutes ago is, first work for Germans. After that, maybe if there is some dirt, you can clean it. If there's some scum on the street, you can clean it. Maybe they would like to give foreigners this kind of stuff. They don't see the advantages of foreigners in Germany. They don't respect homosexuals in Germany. They don't respect handicaps in Germany. They are against all that, and I cannot tolerate this, so that's why I'm here." His voice cracks with upset again as more NPD martial music fills the air.

Greifswald counterdemonstrator

"It's not a real danger," he says. The thuggish-looking marchers don't jeopardize life for most people in Germany, "but it's too dangerous for some persons to live here in Germany, and that's dangerous enough. I don't think that there will ever be a movement like in the thirties or forties in Germany. But right now in Germany's democracy, we can't tolerate even this kind of fascism, though it's the minority."

"But doesn't democracy mean that these people have the right to make this march and to say what they believe?" I yell above the crowd noise.

"Well, that's why they are allowed to do it. I mean, the mayor of this town said, 'I will forbid this demonstration.' But the judge said, 'It's not possible to forbid it because we live in a democracy, and this party, the NPD, is not now forbidden, so I have to allow it.' Well, that's a good sign. So we," he says about the counterdemonstrators, "are forced to show we are against it. We have to show we are a majority. I hope we are."

"Should the NPD be banned?" I wonder.

"I don't know if that's the right way. You should perhaps just isolate them and make the people see how silly they are, how silly their major ideas are."

And what is his message for Jews in the former Soviet bloc who are considering a move to Germany and who see this demonstration on television?

"Well, I'm not really sure if I would like to live in Germany if I saw these pictures," he says as the martial music blares on. "But if everyone settles outside of Germany, this kind of shit will stay here. If Jews come, if foreigners come, we can make Germany more colorful. They should not think this is the real Germany. It's a part of Germany, but it's not *the* Germany."

A common sign on storefronts in Germany shows a profile of a dog and reads *Wir müssen draussen bleiben*, We must stay outside. Around Greifswald an amended version is posted. It features a swastika and a drawing of a dog tied up next to a tethered neo-Nazi, and the words, "We must stay outside." The headline of the poster says, "A sweet pair!" It's an advertisement for a local nightclub.

As I leave the city center of Greifswald I encounter a middle-aged local resident on a quiet street.

"Do you have angst for your city?" I ask him.

His answer is a quick and certain "No!" But he adds, "There is a problem, that's for sure."

"And the solution?"

"That's very difficult. It's important to show civil courage and not to flinch. The NPD is a phenomenon in this region but not only in this region. I think it will shrink if we stand fast for democracy."

He's a Greifswald psychologist who knows skinheads well; his work puts him in direct contact with them, and he's worried. I ask him if he believes they are dangerous.

"Yes, they are dangerous. But only if they are together. By themselves they are mostly not dangerous."

I ask him what advice he would give a Jewish colleague considering a position in Greifswald. "Oh, I think the safest place in Germany is farther west, not in this region." He gives a helpless shrug.

Down the street is a Red Cross station, ready to help with any injuries. A new banner flies in front of the office: *Unser Kreuz hat keine Haken,* Our cross has no hook. The swastika is a *Hakenkreuz* in German, a hooked cross.

I find dinner, and refuge from the strife, at a Greek restaurant.

WHILE neo-Nazis parade, for those who stay home there is familiar theme music on television, announcing a show that has generated further debate: Does it ease or exacerbate the social tensions provoked by neo-Nazis in the street?

As the music fades and the titles roll, instead of Colonel Klink and Sergeant Schultz yelling at each other in English with their caricatures of a German accent, the two buffoons and their cohorts really are speaking German. Every night at seven, across Germany, more than a million viewers are tuning into the Kabel Eins network and watching reruns of *Hogan's Heroes,* the 1960s comedy set in a German prisoner-of-war camp. Most of the audience is under fifty—born after World War II—and making fun of the Nazi era is no taboo for them. Robert Kopf, who produces the German version of the show for Kabel Eins, credits its new success to the changed dialogue: the German translators have made the Nazi characters' lines even more foolish than what was written for the original show.

"So everyone who watches it now—and they have also added laugh tracks, which is very important in my opinion—is clearly aware that this isn't drama, this is comedy, this is a fictional setting. These guys are caricatures, and the Americans and the other prisoners—they are just poking fun at false authorities."

The 168 episodes of *Hogan's Heroes* played successfully around the world before finally finding an audience in Germany, but the show flopped in its first incarnation here with a literal translation of the original American-written lines. What finally is making German viewers laugh is the sight and sound of Nazis acting incomprehensibly idiotic—and that worries some Germans, like Jan Luther, a Berlin student of Prussian history.

"We know that prisoner-of-war camps of Allied soldiers were not filled with happiness and show biz. Many people died there. The National Socialists killed people in those camps; the situation was not as benign as it is portrayed in this series. I think it is not good to show such a thing on TV in Germany."

In fact Luther, who grew up in East Germany, believes that showing *Hogan's Heroes* in Germany is dangerous. In Germany there is no absolute right to free speech. For example, denying the Holocaust is a serious federal crime, and Jan Luther believes it should also be illegal to broadcast *Hogan's Heroes* to a German audience.

"I think it's a way of destroying real history. With comedy you can make a mental break, so that people see it as part of history—it was fun and bad times all mixed up, and they will believe what they want to believe, and not necessarily the truth."

Nonsense, says Kopf at Kabel Eins. The show doesn't distort history. He also rejects criticism from aging German soldiers who claim it defames them and their dead colleagues.

"I don't think our audience is so stupid as to lose contact with reality. I think they are clearly aware of the fact that what the Nazis did was undoubtedly cruel. I think you could compare the show with *M*A*S*H* in America."

Germans often get themselves in trouble with foreigners when they seek to compare Nazi times with other historical examples. Not only is *M*A*S*H* about a hospital camp, but the Americans in Korea were, of course, part of a United Nations force—not a rogue regime leading a nation in crimes against humanity. But history is one thing and commerce is another. Kabel Eins runs *M*A*S*H* and *Hogan's Heroes* back-to-back, managing to build an audience that stays with the network for both shows.

15 □ *Another Jewish Cemetery Is Desecrated*

A COUPLE OF MONTHS after the huge Berlin demonstration, the three-hundred-year-old Jewish cemetery in suburban Potsdam is firebombed. I meet with Potsdam's Rabbi Malcolm Pressman at the charred synagogue in the cemetery. He's a rosy-cheeked cherub of a man. With his big black hat, long black greatcoat, and scraggly beard, he looks the part of an Eastern European rabbi from centuries past, except for the cell phone stuck to his ear. His voice is low and distressed as we survey the damage: minimal to the structures but critical to his heart. We talk adjacent to a plaque that lists—in pre-Nazi-era German Gothic type—members of the Potsdam Jewish community who gave their lives "to their German Fatherland" in the army of Kaiser Wilhelm during World War I. Nearby is a display of newspaper clippings reporting earlier desecrations of the cemetery.

"They told me it was a fire," he says about the first telephone report he received from police. "I was shocked because I didn't expect something like this." Not that the cemetery wasn't a target before this latest attack. "Like I said, until today it was just graffiti, and no big damage." He surveyed the damage. "For a few hours I couldn't speak. I couldn't believe it."

The rabbi tells me that the arsonists, who left a note describing themselves as members of a neo-Nazi organization, drilled a hole in one of the doors, poured in gasoline, and lit it. Although

139

the fire fizzled, the hall reeks of smoke. "To make this place right again," he says, "it's a lot of work, it costs a lot of money."

We talk about perpetrators of the crime. Any crazy person can throw a bomb and leave a note claiming to be part of an organization, we muse. This incident doesn't necessarily mean that Potsdam is home to a neo-Nazi movement. He agrees with that logic in principle. "I think it's crazy people, but I'm sure that the crazy people are not working alone. Because it's an ideology. I don't think it's just because they want to have fun. Sure it's crazy people, but with an ideology." He's using the word "ideology" as a metaphor for the historical problems between Jews and Germans, and he says the NPD feeds contemporary impressionable minds not just with its anti-

Rabbi Malcolm Pressman

foreigner and anti-Semitic propaganda but also with a sense of empowerment and authorization to commit violent acts. "I think this ideology has been in Germany for all time." Even if the schools have taught tolerance since the end of World War II, he says, education doesn't stop at the classroom door. "In a lot of homes, the fathers say to the sons, 'All our problems are from the Jews.' And then the son goes and does something. I am sure there are people here who think every day, all our problems are from the Jews."

Overall things have improved since the war, he says, for all "normal people," but fifty years is not enough time for this anti-Semitic mentality to disappear. "A lot of the German people believe in the ideology." I ask Rabbi Pressman if the firebombing makes him question the wisdom of reestablishing the Jewish community in Germany. "It's a very difficult question. We don't find an answer. We don't know. But for me, I came from Israel because there are Jews here. When Jews choose to live in Germany, I cannot say, 'Hey people, go away from Germany.' This is their life here. So as a religious man, I came and I offer all the services I can. But all the while I think: Why do we need to live in such a country?"

Rabbi Pressman, even as he stands in his wrecked sanctuary, maintains hope. "There are many good people in Germany today." He's lived and worked in Germany for more than five years, often speaking at schools. He sees generational change as students study the Holocaust, travel to Amsterdam to see the Anne Frank house, visit concentration camps. "The children begin to understand that Jews are people, normal people like any others. Then they understand," he looks over at the burned door, "that there's no reason to do this."

Some of those students got in touch with the rabbi after the fire, telling him they were organizing a march to demonstrate their solidarity with the Potsdam Jewish community and their rejection of the neo-Nazis in their midst. "That gives me hope that it's another Germany."

We leave the sanctuary and walk among the headstones and their Hebrew inscriptions. The cemetery is on the outskirts of Potsdam. It's quiet except for the birdsongs. A couple of the police officers now assigned guard duty at the cemetery inspect the damage. The white "Polizei" in stark letters across the backs of their jackets contrasts with the blackened walls.

Rabbi Pressman's optimism is not shared by the cab driver who picks me up at the cemetery for the ride back to the Potsdam train station. He is animated in his disgust with skinheads and neo-Nazis in Potsdam, insisting the problem is worse than officials recognize or admit. Waving his hands in irritation as he talks, looking almost as much at me in the rearview mirror as at the traffic, he tells me he's in a better position than most to see what's happening on the streets. "I've thrown some people out of my taxi. They open the door, young people. They come in and say, 'Heil Hitler! We want to go to . . .' And I say, 'You can walk there. I'm not taking you with me.' It's the truth. I get this regularly. It's bad. I speak only from my experience. They have short hair and nothing in their heads. You wonder what's going on in their heads. They're nineteen, some only eighteen."

My cab driver is worried. Living in Communist East Germany taught him that banning anything, such as the NPD, is not the answer to a threat, because what is outlawed becomes even more attractive. He echoes what the rabbi reports regarding the negative influences in the homes of too many susceptible youngsters. That, coupled with unemployment and the propaganda of neo-Nazi parties such as the NPD, contributes to the offensive behavior he sees in his cab, behavior he's convinced is a sign of much more serious problems, such as the firebombing at the cemetery.

Taxi driver

A FEW DAYS LATER Potsdam police, the mayor, and the public school teachers and their students offer their answer to Rabbi Pressman's question about the future of his Jewish community. They march by the thousands from downtown Potsdam to the cemetery. It is a sunny and bright but chilly winter day as the crowd gathers, anxious to talk about their mission. "I want to show people that I do not agree with the situation in Brandenburg and in Potsdam with the Nazis here," one clean-cut high schooler with a baseball cap on his head tells me earnestly. "We have very many Nazis. You heard about the graveyard, and you know, they have burned the synagogue. I just want to protest against that situation, and I want to show that there's something different, that not everybody who is a teenager is a Nazi."

I ask him if he really fears that Potsdam and Brandenburg are havens for neo-Nazis, and his answer comes without hesitation. "Yes, yes. I see it every day. In the newspapers they often say the situation is not so bad, but that's stupid. I see it every day. I see the problems here in Potsdam, for example at the main train station. There are so many Nazis there. They sit there and drink their beer, and everyone who is black, who looks alternative, is in danger there. The police do nothing about that." How does he know these drunks are neo-Nazis? "I know it because they have signs on their jackets, *Ich bin stolz ein Deutscher zu sein*, I am proud to be German." Although such nationalistic sentiment is common and harmless in most countries, *Ich bin stolz ein Deutscher zu sein* is often still a code for right-wing nationalists in Germany. The high schooler has more examples: "They scream words like '*Sieg Heil*' and '*Ausländer raus!*' Things like that, normal things for them. If you are there late in the evening, you are not safe."

Potsdam demonstrator

He is a delegate from his history class, officially authorized by the school to demonstrate—"to show all people that I have a problem with this situation, that I don't agree with neo-fascism. That I think different." He shares the concern of my taxi driver. "The future looks bad. At this moment it looks really bad. Some parts of the town are no-go areas for blacks, for alternative-looking people, for just anyone who doesn't think like them." He speaks from experience. A few months ago his appearance was different: long hair and "alternative looking," as he puts it. "It's very dangerous, people are not safe there," he says, especially in the more remote Brandenburg villages. "Every day I heard people screaming at me. Often I had to run away. It was dangerous. I was very afraid of them." He looks around at the growing crowd of demonstrators. "Yeah, it's good, but it's just a small part," he says about the Potsdam population. "Many teenagers are not here. Many think, 'No, I won't go.'" Then a cynical smile, "Many are here because they don't have to go to school today. Many don't think about what this demonstration is for. Many are just here thinking, 'Oh, I don't have school. Cool. So I'll go.'"

Potsdam demonstrator

Around us the street is filling with students, most burdened with their backpacks, some listening to music on headphones, others smiling and chatting, all waiting for the march to begin. An organizer with a bullhorn tells me, "We are demonstrating against the right, and we hope that all people in Potsdam stand up against it." With the police diverting traffic to make a path for the students, the march begins, stretching for blocks, filling the downtown streets.

As the marchers turn into the narrow lane approaching the desecrated cemetery, Brandenburg Police Chief Michael Gellenbeck is pleased. "It shows that even the pupils, the kids and the young people here, are on the right side." He realizes immediately that the word "right" can be misinterpreted, laughs, and adds, "Not on the right side but on the side of Jewish people and on the side of the law, and I think that's a good sign."

Chief Gellenbeck tells me he is convinced that Brandenburg is no hotbed of neo-Nazi activity. "Oh, of course it's not, it's definitely not," he insists, shaking his head. He dismisses the problems as almost a fad. "We have towns here where it's kind of a trend. They think it's nice to have short hair and boots, but I don't think this is a general movement in society." The chief stands tall in his brown police uniform, in charge. Townspeople greet him, and his smile comes easily. English comes easily for him too. He's spent time working with colleagues in America. As we talk he compares the skinheads in his jurisdiction with the leftist protests of the sixties. "I think this is a countermovement. Young people always want something else." I point out to him that in the late sixties and seventies the German police harshly and successfully suppressed violent protests. Will they do the same to the extreme right? "Of course we're going to," he says. "We will not accept any violence. We will not accept bringing people fear."

Police Chief Gellenbeck insists his force is after the lawbreakers in Brandenburg and that the state will prosecute them aggressively. "My message is that we have a Jewish community of eight thousand people. Most all of them live here without any problems. Whenever we discover any sort of harassment or violence, we're going to act as powerfully as possible. I don't think there is extreme danger here. Definitely not."

Further, I ask, what is your message to the criminals who did this job in the cemetery?

"I'll tell them that we're going to find them, and there will be a sanction, of course, and I think it will be a hard one. Yeah. I'm sure."

But many of the marchers disagree with the chief. The chatter and laughs cease as the crowd nears the burned building and wanders in front of the cemetery gates. Some hold banners, others carry picket signs.

I catch up with a couple of high school girls, Anna and Jasmine. "There are many people who are right wing," Anna insists, "and the number is growing. It's gotten worse. Many people are against foreigners. We're helping to fight against that."

"You say it's getting worse?" I check to make sure I correctly understand her German.

"Yes, it's a big problem in Germany. It keeps getting worse."

Jasmine tries to explain what type of person she believes could firebomb a cemetery.

"Some come from a background with that philosophy. And they try some little attack."

"In the last ten years, about a hundred people have been murdered by the right," adds Anna. "Something has to be done in response."

What should be done?

"That's a hard question." She agrees that the demonstration is positive. "Yes, I think the community is pulling together and saying something happened here. People are against it."

But Jasmine has a ready response for specific action. "When you see it on the street, you must speak up. If Jews or foreigners are attacked, you have to help them instead of looking the other direction and running away."

As the demonstrators head back toward downtown, Rabbi Pressman shows the burn marks to the mayor.

"We shouldn't belittle the problem," the mayor says. "It's debated in kitchens and cafés. There is a militant xenophobia that a few base their beliefs on. There's an anti-Semitic faction opposed to both residents and immigrants. It's a philosophy that's generally rejected. We're dealing with a small group that we must be careful of, it is not a sentiment shared by 90 percent of the population. You saw today that the vast majority will not tolerate this any longer. Many issues are still tied to the former East Germany—the lack of education, the lack of work, the lack of perspective. We must deal with these issues."

The mayor says the schools must teach tolerance at an earlier age and stress the facts of the Holocaust. But for Rabbi Pressman, this day is a blessing. He's smiling when I find him just outside the damaged sanctuary and ask him about the demonstration.

"It's very helpful. It soothes our feelings. Like we said yesterday, we felt damaged, and now it's a lot better."

"Are you optimistic or pessimistic about the future now?" I ask.

"I'm optimistic, sure. A rabbi must be optimistic. There are so many children here. They're the future of this city, so we cannot be anything but optimistic."

16 □ *Escalating Neo-Nazi Crimes*

JOURNALIST FRANK JANSEN watches and worries. He's been studying right-wing violence in Germany for well over a dozen years, and his research has forced the government to acknowledge that the problem is far worse than was originally stated by officials. He's documented upward of one hundred people killed by neo-Nazis and skinheads, scores more injured, extensive property damage. The German nation finally is alarmed. Jansen is one of the few German journalists assigned to report on the extremist right. His stories have revealed that the crimes committed by neo-Nazis and skinheads have been not just random violence but politically motivated hate crimes. His reporting has forced major changes in national politics and law enforcement techniques. Before the publication of his dispatches from the front lines of the neo-Nazi assaults, the government had not acknowledged the true dimensions of the right-wing threat nor taken any serious action to combat it. His work has forced Germans to look into their dark side once again.

DATELINE, BERLIN. From the *New York Times*: "A firebomb badly damaged a Holocaust museum near the northeast German town of Wittstock, the Brandenburg State police said today." The story rated just a few paragraphs in the paper. "Half the museum's exhibition space was destroyed, and swastikas and anti-Semitic graffiti were painted in pink on a nearby monument's walls." Some of the graffiti required interpretation, reported the paper. "The vandals also painted an anti-Semitic slogan, 'Jews have short legs,' a twist on the German saying that 'lies have short legs.' [The museum's spokesman] said the intended message was that 'the Holocaust is a lie.'"

In the years following German reunification, similar reports became almost commonplace news items.

FRANK JANSEN writes for Berlin's *Tagesspiegel* newspaper. Since his exposés on the extent of neo-Nazi violence in Germany, he lives under constant threat of death and with police protection. When police uncovered the plot to kill Jansen, they felt it was credible enough to warn him, offer him police protection, and suggest that he vary his daily routine considerably in order to make an attack more difficult. In the Jansen case, police discovered a sniper rifle and written material indicating that Jansen was the target.

Frank Jansen does not hide his loathing for the neo-Nazis. "In Brandenburg," he says about the state that surrounds Berlin and is such a hotbed of skinhead violence, "fewer than 2 percent are foreigners. But the residents there think there are many more. When you go to a town and ask, people say, 'Oh, there are thousands!' when there are only about two hundred. The increase is in their minds." It is this fear of outsiders that the NPD takes advantage of as the party tries to influence Germans, especially the frustrated young unemployed in the former East Germany. "Some in the NPD really are radical," Jansen notes, "and talk about riots, saying someday there will be riots in the East. One of the leaders of the NPD said to me in 1999, 'In five years we will have a great riot in Germany.' And that was not a joke."

We meet at the *Tagesspiegel* offices just as the paper's huge, high-speed presses begin to turn out the next day's editions, and talk about the work that has consumed him since just after German reunification. Jansen is a lean, soft-spoken, mild-mannered man with blue penetrating eyes that give the impression of exhaustion from seeing so much pain and perversity. He peppers his fluent English with asides to make clear both his abject disgust with the perpetrators of right-wing violence and his frequent frustration with the authorities who are charged with keeping the peace in his country. His stories prove that the real number of acts of illegal political violence continues to be larger than what the government officially acknowledges.

"I think one of the main causes is the reunification with all its consequences. When it came in 1990, you saw that both in West and East Germany you had a great lack of democracy. In East Germany because of forty years of communism, and before that twelve years of National Socialism. But also a lack of democracy in West Germany, where democracy was presented as just another word for prosperity. But prosperity didn't come at once for East Germans,

Frank Jansen

as Chancellor Helmut Kohl said it would in 1990. What came was that people lost their jobs, people became very afraid."

As the cradle-to-grave guarantees of basic food, clothing, and shelter provided for forty years by the old East German government ended, and unemployment and prices soared, millions of former East Germans grew despondent.

"So," Jansen tells me, "they said, 'Okay, if this is democracy, we don't want it at all.' But they didn't want to go back to communism either. The youngsters felt there must be an alternative." For a considerable number of these frustrated and alienated youngsters, the Nazi era seems to offer that alternative. Jansen says they find it easy to romanticize and idealize Adolf Hitler and the Nazis. "Twelve years of National Socialism, new military successes in the Second World War, and with that marching, people in the streets, shouting, screaming." Fears of

150

the future that fuel the Nazi nostalgia of these youngsters find common cause with similarly frustrated pensioners. "Many of the elderly in East Germany were really afraid of the few foreigners who came as refugees to East Germany after reunification—the asylum seekers." The neo-Nazi leaders took advantage of this brewing discontent. "There was a very sharp mixture of frustration, aggression, disappointment." As a result, explains Jansen, "People said, 'We don't like democracy,' and the youngsters said, 'Okay, let's fight democracy. Let's fight the foreigners. Let's fight for a Fourth Reich.' "

I recount to Frank Jansen stories about the civic leaders and the men and women on the street I've talked with throughout Germany who dismiss the marauding street toughs as just drunk kids who don't have jobs, are not well educated, and have no real ideology. They're just drunk, I keep hearing, and they're acting out neo-Nazi roles without understanding the historical background of their behavior.

"That's not true," Jansen says emphatically. "Of course there are some young skinheads who have no jobs and are on the dole. But in most cases, when I go to court and see them sitting there accused of murder, physical assault, and the like, many of them still go to school or have a job, or they're living with their parents. Some of them come with their own cars. They're well dressed." He shakes his head. "In most cases it's not true that they are poor people without jobs who have to fight for their existence. Most of them, I guess, are bored, and that's why they're ready for skinhead music too." But Jansen is convinced their actions are not random and often find familial support. "In the morning their parents say to them, 'We don't like these foreigners here, the foreigners are taking jobs away from East Germans.' In the evening the youngsters say, 'Okay, we've got good reasons to push the foreigners out,' to do some Paki-bashing, as they say in London. There is a direct link between the so-called normal racism in the population and the right-wing violence of the young people."

Frank Jansen rejects the notion that unemployment drives the bigotry and violence. "In fact it's only one reason. I think there are many, many more reasons." Finding work for eastern Germany's jobless will not end the violence, he says. "After fifty-six years of dictatorship, people are not ready for a democratic system, finding compromises, looking for tolerance. They are not ready to look for another way of life." When prosperity did not come immediately with reunification in 1990, be believes, many eastern Germans began looking for solutions in the authoritarian experiences of their recent history. At the same time, Jansen fears, the government continues to minimize the crises in the East. "The authorities don't want to see this problem. They say, 'These are only kids, and this racist prejudice—oh, it's not so bad, not so prevalent, only a few people.' They're very afraid of having a bad image in the United States, Western Europe, and around the world. They're really afraid that investors will not come to eastern Germany. So the political class is not engaged." Instead, he says, they blame the messenger. "They say, 'Okay, the media. The media. You are pushing this problem. It's not like this.'"

Meanwhile, far-right politicians seize upon the malcontents for their own purposes. Some attract them with simple slogans such as "Foreigners out, more jobs for Germans." But Jansen puts the National Democratic party in a separate category from most other right-wing extremist organizations because of its sophistication and its goal of changing Germany's political system. "The NPD is different because the NPD seeks out the young people, mainly the skinheads and the neo-Nazis, and tells them we need a totally new system, something very similar to the Third Reich but more anti-capitalist. That's why the NPD is really successful among the youngsters in eastern Germany. They say what we need is a social form of nationalism. But 'social' means to them, in fact, only for Germans. It means kicking out all the foreigners and then being 'social'—giving benefits to the Germans and no one else. And only the *good* Germans, of course. So the NPD is really successful among the skinheads. But it is not successful in elections because its marches, its demonstrations remind a lot of people of the marches of the Nazis or the SA or the SS."

I ask Jansen if he's uncovered any evidence of the NPD leadership instructing its skinhead cadres to engage in street violence, or if the skinheads jump to that conclusion themselves based on the NPD's propaganda.

"The jump's already under way," he says, pointing to the firebombing of the Jewish cemetery in Potsdam. "The NPD program is, as you say, grass roots, that's quite true. They say, 'We start with the youngsters. The youngsters will get older, and then we can gain a larger base in the whole population.' And they say, 'Okay, that will take a long time. We know that, that's okay.' They say it's necessary to fight for the streets and then fight for the parliaments. But more important for them is fighting for the streets—win the streets, win the young skinheads. And among the youngsters they're quite successful."

The connection between the thugs on the street and the NPD offices is via code words and what Jansen calls political training. "Political training means saying to the people, 'What you want is a new system, and you have to look to the past, to what was good about the past.' These are easy-to-break codes designed to sanitize and rehabilitate Nazi philosophies." Concurrent with the successes of the NPD and other far-right political activists has been the ongoing exodus of Jewish immigrants to Germany from the former Soviet Union and the former Soviet bloc. I ask Jansen if he sees a connection between the increase in neo-Nazi skinhead right-wing activities and this immigration. His answer is both gratifying and disconcerting.

"I don't think there is a really close connection between the growth of the Jewish community and the increase in neo-Nazi activities, because the neo-Nazis and the skinheads would act even if there were no increase. What you see in Brandenburg or the other so-called new states in Germany is a very small percentage of foreigners. Brandenburg has fewer than 2 percent foreigners. But people hate foreigners. They think there are many, many more. This increase is in their mind."

Jansen tells the story of a small village in Brandenburg where the German immigration authorities decided to temporarily relocate some 150 immigrating Jews onto the estate of a former noble family. The townsfolk wanted nothing to do with the newcomers; they wanted the government to send them elsewhere. Jansen raises his eyebrows as he tells the story. "The people were very, very angry there. And the prime minister of Brandenburg said, 'Okay, I can understand the people.' He was harshly criticized, mainly by the Jewish community in Germany. After that I guess the authorities thought, okay, maybe we'd better bring the Jews to Berlin and not to Brandenburg."

Of course the unsophisticated skinheads who make trouble in the streets find it easier to pick a student from Somalia or a merchant from Turkey out of a crowd than to find a Jew. Many Germans from the East grew up without much opportunity to meet Jews—Jews whose outward appearances, naturally, may well match their own. Jansen considers Brandenburg and the other new German states not just dangerous for Jews and foreigners but for outspoken Germans like himself.

"I think it would not be safe for me to live there, because neo-Nazis know me. They hate me, and in the new states it would be easier for them to attack me than here in Berlin. I'm German," he smiles. "I'm Aryan, blue eyes"—he points to his eyes—"blond hair"—he grabs a lock of it—making it clear that he believes the threats are real even for someone who matches the skinheads' stereotypes for acceptability. "I think for foreigners it's getting more and more dangerous." He tells the story of a computer start-up company that is located in Frankfurt Oder, on the Polish border with eastern Germany. The company employed specialists from India, Iran, and Spain. Six months after they went into business, Jansen received a call from the plant manager imploring him to come east. "He said, 'You should come to Frank-furt Oder. Every one of my new employees has been attacked. Everybody has been attacked. Everybody there.' That's the situa-tion." Jansen sighs and rolls his eyes.

Jansen is convinced that the slow response of politicians to the rise of right-wing extremism makes the assaults and vandal-ism hard to quell. "There's no ending. We have some special units of the police designed to fight right-wing extremism. But we need to change the minds of the people, to get rid of this racist thinking. That's the most important thing." What he calls "normal racism" fuels the street violence despite the special po-lice. "Normal racism—it means that most of the people in East Germany will say, 'Foreigners out!' They would say the NPD is a normal party. They would say we don't need Jews here. Or they would say we have too many foreigners here."

This "normal racism" is exacerbated by teachers and police left over from East Germany, teachers ill-trained regarding Ger-man responsibility for the Holocaust, and some police who share the prejudices of the lawbreakers. "In East Germany it's important to talk directly to the people. If you have an incident in a small city, maybe a foreigner's been beaten and people say, 'That's okay, we don't need them here.' Politicians—maybe the prime minister or someone who is very well known—must go there for a public meeting. The politician must say, 'You can tell me what you think about foreigners, and I will tell you the facts and something about morality. I will tell you that this is not good for you, not good for us, not good for our jobs, and not good for our economy.' They *should* do it, but they haven't done it." As an example he cites the arson destruction of a complex for asylum seekers in a Brandenburg village in 1992. The place was torched the day before it was to be occupied, so there were no injuries. But because it was destroyed, the arsonists were able to prevent another village from being forced to host the for-eigners. Jansen laments the failure to act of Germany's politicians. "No one went there to talk to the people and say, 'What have you done? To Brandenburg, to our country. What have you done?' No one did it."

To what does he attribute this lack of action? Is it naiveté, is it disinterest?

"I guess it's disinterest. But it's also fear, because it's quite unpopular to talk about this situation. I think a lot of people in politics say, 'We have so many problems, why must I, especially, go to these people and investigate what's happening? Maybe someone else can do that.'" He takes a deep breath. "I'm really concerned. I think the problem will grow. Perhaps the numbers will decline, but the degree of violence will worsen. I'm concerned that we will have terrorism—primitive terrorism, but it's also dangerous. And I think the threat will rise." He looks off into the distance. "I'm not sure this society is prepared to say that more than a huge demonstration is needed. We need strategies for many years, not just for a couple of months. It's necessary not only to ban the party, it's necessary to change minds."

Is the country in jeopardy?

"I don't think it's in jeopardy as in 1933." He does not fear the government will be overthrown, but he sees a civil society already in danger. "The threat is growing so large that some people may decide to leave this country, to emigrate because they cannot live safely here. You see this situation in the new states. Foreigners with dark skin, those who look quite Jewish—as people think Jews should look—it's not safe for them. We have some places where you can sense it's a no-go area." Jansen describes typical no-go areas in the anonymous-looking housing blocks that dot urban eastern Germany. "You see the youngsters in their cars or walking around with shaved heads. You see them looking, watching you." He nods his head slowly. "You know what's going on."

Frank Jansen reports from these no-go areas.

"They don't understand me. I'm not trying to tell them what I think is right. I'm just asking questions. I'll ask, 'What kind of political system should Germany have?' They'll say, 'Something like National Socialism.' And when I ask them, 'What do you think about Auschwitz? What do you think about concentration camps?' they'll say, 'Maybe it works.' I've talked with a lot of youngsters. I don't think I can change their minds. It's really necessary to change the minds of the parents, the teachers, the policemen, so they can say to the youngsters, 'You have to change. You have to stop this violence.' But I'm still waiting for this to happen."

I tell Jansen about my chat with the taxi driver who took me back to the Potsdam train station from the firebombed cemetery.

"He was what you might call a 'normal' Brandenburger," I say. "He was incensed, talking to me about how upset he was by what had happened. Isn't this an example of that change you're waiting for?"

"When people are confronted directly with violence they are shocked," he says. "When they see houses burned and people lying there in their blood, they are shocked, of course. But after that, when you talk to them and you ask them, 'What do you think? Are there too many foreigners here in Germany?' they say, 'Yes, of course.' They don't see a contradiction." Jansen tells of another case, a story he covered in Brandenburg. A Turkish-owned snack bar was burned down by skinheads and neo-Nazis. After Jansen's report was published in *Tagesspiegel*, Berliners donated a substantial amount of money to help the proprietor rebuild his business in the Brandenburg provinces. Jansen returned to the scene of the crime with the donations and interviewed local citizens for a follow-up story. Is there prejudice against foreigners here, he asked them? They acknowledged xenophobia in their village.

"I asked them why," Jansen recounts to me, "and they said, 'Oh, there are so many Turks here, and for you in Berlin, there are so many Turks. It's awful, it's awful.'" Jansen throws up his hands in resignation. "What could I say?" He offers a wan smile as he finishes the tale. "Three months after that, this Turkish man decided to leave Germany. I found him and he said to me, 'I was terrorized again, and it was too dangerous.' So he left. That's the situation."

I ask him one of my stock questions. "If you had acquaintances, colleagues, Jewish friends in Uzbekistan or Kazakhstan or St. Petersburg, and they were looking to better themselves and saw the opportunity to come to Germany and start a new life here, what would be your message for them?"

He laughs. "My message would be, maybe it's better to go to the United States or to Israel. Or I could say, 'Okay, you can come to Berlin. Berlin's situation is not as dangerous as in the new states in East Germany.' But," he waves his hands with dismissal, "I could not say to them, 'Okay, come to Brandenburg, it's quite proper, it's quite okay, it's very nice. Easy living, nice people.' I cannot say that. It's not true."

17 □ *Rebuilding Berlin's Jewish Life*

"THE MESSAGE IS against racism, against anti-Semitism, and it gives me a good feeling to be a part of the 200,000." Hermann Simon and I are chatting in his comfortable office at the New Synagogue on Oranienburgerstrasse, the gorgeous domed building that was severely damaged first during *Kristallnacht* and then by Allied bombing during the war. The gilded dome is intact again, reconstructed just as East and West Berlin reunited, topped off with a golden Star of David that shimmers in the Berlin *Luft*. A plaque at the entrance notes this history of destruction and renewal and adds, VERGESST ES NIE, never forget.

Simon is director of the Centrum Judaicum, the foundation that maintains the library, archives, and memorabilia housed in the adjoining buildings, a foundation dedicated to the study of Berlin Jews. We're talking about the massive November 9 march through Berlin's streets. "It's a good feeling to live as a Jew in Germany and to know there are not only right-wingers, that the majority is with me, with us. The Jews. And the foreigners. The black people. That's the message. It's not just the Jews. It was a demonstration against xenophobia. Especially for the Jews. It's a good sign that it started on the 9th of November, here in front of the New Synagogue, with a prayer from the rabbi and then the political speeches at another point, at the Brandenburg Gate." He nods with a contented smile. "Really, it was good. I have seen it. I attended. I received many calls from all over the world. It is a good sign."

We talk about right-wing violence. I tell him of my conversations with Jews such as Leonid Rosenthal, who avoid parts of East Berlin, worried about their safety and security. "He's afraid?" Simon is surprised and irritated. "That's his problem," he says with dismissal. Simon is in his fifties, with short greying hair, dressed in a conservative blue suit. He looks the part of a successful businessman. "Every day I travel by underground, by S-Bahn, by streetcar. I never go by car because I haven't a car. I think many people know me," he shrugs modestly. "It is a face many people know. I have no problems." But beyond Berlin, he acknowledges, is another story. "There are some places in Brandenburg, for example, that are dangerous for black people." But for a Jew? "I have no problems," he says, and then switches back to German and says it again. *Ich habe keine Angst.*" He points out the advantage he has over Leonid Rosenthal and other recent immigrants. "My language is German. I speak better German than any other language in the world. I know Russian and English very well. But my mother tongue is German. I was born here. *Ich bin ein Berliner,*" he laughs.*

Hermann Simon was born just after the war, in the Jewish Hospital in the French sector of occupied Berlin. When he was just days old, he began life across the artificial lines drawn in the city, in the Russian sector. He became a citizen of the German Democratic Republic. He grew up in East Berlin, a member of the tiny Jewish community there, a community that was dying out. The resurgence of that community makes him happy. "I think it is a great future, we have a future. I remember very well 10, 12 years ago when we had 203 members." He says each word precisely, recalling the exact figure with a wry smile, "There were two or three children, I can't remember. But there was no prospect of a Jewish community in all of the country.

*The famous John F. Kennedy line is embraced with fondness by Berliners who heard the president's speech in 1963. Over the years the line has drawn amusement from those who know of the regional Berlin sweet—essentially a jelly donut—called a *Berliner*.

Now we have a future as Jews in Germany, as a Jewish community. Not only as one Jewish community, as a *Jüdishegemeinschaft*, as we say in German. There is a future. We have schools, we have institutions. I have a hope for the future of Jewish life in Berlin, in Germany. Otherwise I wouldn't stay. There is a future, I am sure. I strongly feel it."

"Tell me why," I encourage him.

"Why not? It's a typical Jewish answer. There are some hundred thousand—I don't know how many Jews we are now in Germany, but in Berlin we have twelve thousand."

That the new Jews are mostly from the former Soviet Union and now constitute a majority of Berlin Jews doesn't bother this German, though he is somewhat troubled by the lack of linguistic assimilation he hears from the newcomers. "It means the common language in our community is Russian." Officially Jewish Berlin is bilingual. The Jewish community's newspaper is published in both languages. "It's not the right way to integrate." But Simon is patient. He sighs when I ask if the German Jews are embracing this influx. "Let's wait ten years. In ten years I will give you an answer. Nobody knows. I think it will be a new community. Nowadays it is more Russian. But we have many Americans. We have also some Israelis. Berlin is a melting pot, and so is the Jewish community."

"Is it a real melting pot here?"

"I think so. I think so."

I point out the armored personnel carrier parked in front of his ornate historic building, with the machine gun mounted on its cab and the patrolling police cradling their machine guns. I mention the metal detector and the search required to get into his offices. Those aren't the signs of a peaceful melting pot.

"Yup, yup," he nods. "It isn't normal. I would be happy if we didn't need the guards. But the authorities charged with security tell us, 'You need the guards.' That's it." Another shrug. "It's not normal. I agree with you. And in the end it isn't good."

161

"But is it necessary? Does it suggest danger for Jews in Berlin?"

"I don't know. You'll have to ask the officials. I told you: *Ich habe keine Angst*. I don't need them. But when the security authorities in this city say it's necessary, the Jewish community can't say it is not necessary. Because then if, God forbid, something happens, who would be responsible? That's the problem."

I ask Simon about the attacks against foreigners and Jews, when swastikas are spray-painted and Jewish graves desecrated. "Is that mindless violence, or is it ideologically motivated?"

"I think personally it is ideologically motivated," says Hermann Simon. "These are not children, playing like children. It is motivated by some bloody ideas."

Of course there is anti-Semitism in France, in Denmark, in Sweden, in Kansas. "Is it different when it occurs in Germany because of the Nazi past?"

"It's not my problem," he says of the other locales. "My problem is anti-Semitism in Germany. As we all know, something happened in Germany—a little bit more than in the United States. We live here, and we will stay here, and we have to take care."

Life in Berlin is good for him, says Simon. "That's my joy," to be a Jew in Berlin and no longer worry about finding enough coreligionists for a minyan when it's time for services. "It's a good feeling for me. I like to live, and I like to live in Berlin. I'm proud to be a Jew, and I'm proud to be a German Jew. I'm proud to be a Berliner. *Ich bin ein Berliner*—I can say it with a Berliner pronunciation, not with an American accent!"

CHRISTIAN DERKS, curator of the archives at the Centrum Judaicum, shows me a handwritten note, scrawled on a scrap of paper in the distinctive cursive still taught in German primary schools. "It says, 'Papa! We've been collected. Come immediately to the collection camp, to the Grosse Hamburgerstrasse in

Berlin.'* And it's signed by Klaus and his mama." Historian Derks handles the note carefully, wearing a white cotton glove. Klaus and his mama, as well as his papa, survived the war as Jews. "The writer of this note was a sixteen-year-old, Klaus. The Gestapo came to their home, here in Berlin *Mitte*, and took Klaus and mama to the collection camp, and said they should go to Theresienstadt. The father later came home and saw this note. He went to the collection camp and took Klaus and his wife out of the camp grounds. It was possible because the father was a kind of policeman in the collection camp." But the family enjoyed only a short respite. "Later they were deported to Theresienstadt." There they lived through the war, the father again assuming the role of a *Ordner*, an enforcer for the Nazis.

"We put these documents and photos together to show what really happened here in Germany, and not long ago," says Derks. There is a stark immediacy to Klaus's note. It looks so familiar and mundane—like a reminder tacked to a refrigerator to buy a quart of milk or take out the trash. Derks flips the note. It's written on paper from the pad of a doctor's office, Dr. M. Goldstein, a neurologist with an office on Dresdenerstrasse. "Especially young people can see that this happened and it's real." Using personal artifacts such as Klaus's note, Christian Derks organized an exhibition called "Jews in Berlin, 1938–1945," a show detailing the lives of individual Jews who survived the war in Berlin. The idea was to avoid treating Nazi history as abstract, to make it specific to the stories of real Berliners. "It's very difficult to teach this period to young people. They say, 'Oh, not again. It doesn't concern us.' It's very difficult."

Derks shows me photographs of Jewish businesses defaced with *Juden Raus* graffiti, shop windows covered with Stars of

*The Grosse Hamburgerstrasse was one of the main Jewish streets in prewar Berlin. A retirement home there was used by the Nazis as a detention house from which many Jews were shipped to concentration and extermination camps.

David. He's preserved a sign posted by the Berlin Jewish community at the Jewish cemetery. *Achtung!* it warns. "Do not cross the street to get to the S-Bahn stop because the Gestapo are waiting there and will arrest you." One of the bizarre restrictions placed on Jews as the Nazi abuses escalated prohibited them from crossing the street in front of the Jewish cemetery at Weissensee, thus preventing easy access to public transport. Derks shows me a section of yellow cloth patterned with Stars of David just like the one worn by Horst Gessner. Dotted lines separate the stars, a guide for cutting them out of the bolt. "This is an original fabric of yellow stars, and some of the stars are not here. It was used, as you can see." Portions of the cloth are cut. "They were worn by Jews in Berlin. Every Jew had to buy three stars, three pieces, for ten *Pfennig*. They had to wear a star on the left side of their jacket every time they went out of the house and into public. Every Jew—man, woman, and child from six to sixty-four years—had to wear this mark on the street."

Christian Derks is a relatively young man, steeped in the worst history of his nation. He is fully aware of the surge of right-wing violence staining the new Germany. "It's really crazy, and I can't understand what's going on here. If you see these documents and hear what the old people say—survivors who are still alive—I can't believe it. I can't believe that people don't understand what happened, what crazy horrible things happened here, not far away, just sixty years ago. And that's not very much time." For Derks, who is not a Jew, Germany is not yet normal. "Of course it's not all right if people are afraid to go to the synagogue and policemen have to stand here in front of the door. That's not right, of course not. It's a problem, *ja*."

OLD SYNAGOGUES are being resurrected and new ones built across Germany. Jewish rites of passage—weddings, baby namings, bar and bat mitzvahs abound in Berlin and testify to the rapidly rising Jewish population. The new immigrants are learning fast about their new homeland and their religious heritage.

Many of them speak no German, no English, no Yiddish, and no Hebrew—the common languages of Berlin's older resident Jews. The newcomers require a wide range of help as they struggle to adapt.

Since many Jewish immigrants from the former Soviet Union have little or no training in the Jewish faith, schools such as one set up by the Lauder Foundation in a historic Berlin synagogue teach the fundamentals of Orthodox Judaism. University student Yosie Levine, from Los Angeles, is one of the teachers at the Lauder school. Students in groups of a half-dozen or so sit around tables with tutors, analyzing texts, working aloud in English and German. "Our goal is to reinvigorate the Jewish community here in Germany," Levine explains. He's young, and enthusiastic about his work. "We work teaching and studying Torah. We're trying to give our students the tools to rebuild the Jewish community here."

Yosie Levine and I chat in the modern classroom, shelves lined with books in Hebrew, while his students continue their work. I ask him why he's motivated to come to Germany to teach, why it's important for him to help rebuild a Jewish community in Germany. "The reality is that there are somewhere in the neighborhood of a hundred thousand Jews living in Germany now. A big part of Judaism centers not on the individual but on the community: the synagogue, the school. We want to make Judaism as rich and as full as possible here. That means setting up schools and giving people the opportunity to learn and to know as much as possible about Judaism, so it can be strong and thriving." He raises his voice slightly so I can hear him: he's competing with students chanting recitations at a nearby table.

I point out to Levine the odd mix we're witnessing. He's an American teaching Jews from the former Soviet bloc about Judaism so that they can build a Jewish community in Germany. He says he finds the combination comfortable. "We have a basic tenet in Judaism: every Jew is responsible for one another. That means that we don't pay much attention to denominations or backgrounds or places of origin. That I'm American teaching people of Russian origin here in Germany—I don't think this is a contradiction, because we all share a common history and hopefully a common destiny. We're talking about Torah, which brings all together and unites us all. So it's really an attempt to touch on all those common chords and bridge the community."

Regarding dangers facing the developing Jewish community from Germany's neo-Nazis, Levine is calm and confident. "I think it's all relative, really. I think anytime you pick up and leave your past life behind, you're going to face new challenges just because you're in a new place and you have to deal with a new set of rules and a new set of circumstances. But I don't think that the fact that these Jews are in Germany makes it necessarily harder than anywhere else in Europe. Sixty years after the Holocaust we *are* living amidst a new generation." It's clear he really believes Germany is a changed society. "That's not to say we shouldn't be wary of our past and think about it a lot, but it also shouldn't tell us that building a new Jewish community here is impossible, because I don't think that's true."

He feels personally safe enough living and working in sophisticated Berlin. "I can't say that I have ever felt unsafe or threatened. I read—the same way I might read about a KKK rally when I'm back home in Los Angeles—I read about a neo-Nazi incident in eastern Germany when I'm reading the newspaper here in Berlin. I think world history shows that there are always people on the periphery. There are people out there who don't like us," he smiles and shrugs with acceptance, "and that's always been the case. I don't think it's particular to a region or to a specific people. I think wherever you are, you face that type of problem. It's just another obstacle to overcome, but it shouldn't be insurmountable."

As a teacher, working to rebuild Germany's Jewish community, Yosie Levine sees no reason to debate a future for Jews in Germany. "For my money, the question is easily answered. The reality is, the Jews are here. They are here in large enough numbers for them to be a reality. I don't think you can say, 'It's something we have to talk about.'" He makes a valid point as he dismisses the question: there is no alternative.

Levine also rejects the labeling of newcomers as "butter Jews," immigrating just for economic improvement and with no interest in their religious and ethnic heritage. "I suppose my view is a bit jaded because I work with a very specific group who are genuinely motivated and genuinely interested in knowing more about Judaism and becoming more Jewish. Whether or not that's representative of the majority of Jews living in Germany, I'm not one to make that judgment. Sure, it's always possible that people may just be looking for a free lunch. At the same time, I don't think that takes away from the people who are genuinely motivated and have the right intentions."

His advice for those Soviet-bloc Jews still trying to make up their minds about a move to Germany is to reiterate that it is a new society. "I think that in general the populace here has definitely made strides in the last couple of generations. Berlin happens to be very cosmopolitan and very diverse. There are large Turkish communities, there are large Jewish communities, there are large Russian communities. It's really not the same uniform population you'd find in Munich in 1935. Whether or not that means that everyone who comes here will find a land of opportunity is a different question. But at least the mind-set is not opposed to that philosophy."

One of Levine's colleagues at the school is Reuven Zakheim from Silver Spring, Maryland. He is most satisfied with his work teaching these newcomers from the Soviet bloc because "it's giving these individuals an opportunity to discover why, what it's about, when they have 'Jewish' stamped on their passport. It's an opportunity for them to really understand their background and, if they decide they want to participate in it, to make it something they know about and something they're proud of. Our job is to give them the tools so that they can have that knowledge." Not that it's hardship duty for Zakheim. "It strengthens my faith. It makes me a better person, a better Jew. So it's definitely a two-way street." He grins. "It's not because I'm particularly altruistic. It helps *me* grow religiously."

The Lauder school, funded with money earned from Estee Lauder cosmetics, makes use of quarters on the grounds of the old synagogue in eastern Berlin at Rykestrasse 53, guarded—of course—by machine-gun-toting Berlin police. Schoolchildren and shoppers pass by, giving the police no more notice than a parking meter or a fire hydrant. They are a routine element of the streetscape. The red brick building is decorated above the entryways with intricate colorful mosaics, showing off a sparkling Star of David glowing over the tablets containing the Ten Commandments spelled out in Hebrew. The façade and the tablets' message give the building a distinguished and lasting presence, as does the synagogue's cantor. A Polish survivor of Auschwitz, he's been on the job for more than thirty-seven years when I visit. He ended up in East Germany after the war and has conducted services there since. The synagogue was not destroyed in 1938 on *Kristallnacht*, not because of its elegant brick but because of its proximity to adjacent buildings. The rampaging Nazi mobs were under orders to avoid damaging the shops, offices, and homes of non-Jewish neighbors. But the synagogue was closed in 1942 and used by the Nazis for the duration of the war as a stable. Teachers and pupils in the adjoining school were deported to death camps.

As director of the Lauder Foundation's Berlin operations, American Joel Levy witnesses the integration of the new arrivals at the school. Looking prim and official on the front steps of the synagogue, he too talks of success. "It's possible to live a Jewish life in Germany today. There is a reflourishing of Jewish life taking place here." He enjoys the irony. "Many of the immigrants from the former Soviet Union who come here are discovering their Jewish roots in Germany. It's possible to do that. That may not be the reason to come, but it's possible should they decide to come here."

But, I suggest to him, why Germany? Why discover your Jewish roots in Germany, of all places? You could walk up and down Brighton Beach and people would say, "Germany? You're going to Germany? Why would you possibly want to go to Germany, especially as a Jew?" My own aunt tried to talk me out of just such a visit to Germany.

"There are a number of reasons," says Levy, adding that he doesn't think it's necessarily important to build a Jewish community in Germany, but because one exists it needs to be nurtured. "People have decided to come here. The Jews are living here. If Jews are here, they have the right to a Jewish education and a Jewish life. From my perspective, that's the reason for the work we're trying to do. But people should make their own decisions as to where they want to live. Germany today is a democratic country in which people can have freedom of religion and freedom of conscience. It's one of the leading bastions of democracy in Europe today. Why not? I don't think there is any central plan to repopulate Germany with Jews, but people have chosen to live here and they have the right to lead a Jewish life in the country of their choice. Simple as that."

Joel Levy

Levy agrees that most of the new immigrants are drawn to Germany by its economic opportunities. The fact that German law guarantees Jews immediate entry and lifelong welfare support makes Germany an obvious choice.

"At the same time they're very, very curious about their Jewish heritage, something they couldn't learn about in the former Soviet Union, had no opportunity. We find a tremendous degree of interest on the part of many of these people."

I point to the police patrol and ask about security. Joel Levy says he is concerned about violence and the threat of it, but he counsels patience and even confidence. "I hope the German authorities will continue their efforts to rout out this very small minority of people on the fringe—this scourge of right radicalism—who would have another kind of world than the world most Germans want." Especially in eastern Germany, he says, change isn't always as rapid as we might wish. "This reunification of Germany occurred in 1989—that's a very, very short time in history. And it's a difficult process. We know the Bible story of the forty years in the desert. Some Germans perhaps are still in the desert. It's going to take some time. But the effort has begun and has to continue. The price of democracy is eternal vigilance, as we're so fond of saying in America, and this is being demonstrated in Germany now."

In the meantime, is it dangerous for the pioneers, especially in the remote villages of the former East? "Sometimes," he says with a sigh and a nod, "but in general, not. It's not necessarily easy for some of the people who end up in some of the smaller places. We work with many of these small isolated communities, but I don't think that most of them are, in fact, very endangered."

You're optimistic, I suggest to Joel Levy as we say goodbye. "I'm very optimistic," he almost smiles.

18 □ A Visit with Hitler's New Followers and Their Leader

I CROSS BERLIN, traveling from the optimism of the developing Jewish community east toward a rare inside view of the National Democratic party's headquarters "bunker" and a chance to question its chairman, Udo Voigt. Our meeting occurs as the NPD fights the government's campaign to have the party banned for violating the basic constitutional law against neo-Nazi activism. Just a short drive from the eclectic and resurging Jewish community, I listen as Voigt explains why he believes Jews ought to go to Israel, not come to Germany.

"GERMANY for the Germans! Send the foreigners home! Send the Jews to the Middle East!"

These slogans sound like echoes of the hate-filled words from the founding of Hitler's Third Reich. But in fact they are contemporary. They are the heart of the official platform of one of Germany's most notorious radical right-wing political organizations, the NPD.

Back in the early days of the Hitler era, the Nazis pledged to free their land from the *Untermenschen*, the "subhumans" for whom the Führer blamed most of Germany's problems.

Hitler used simplistic slogans and rallies to build popular support for what would become a policy of racially driven mass murder. Today neo-Nazi skinheads and the political party that recruits them are using similar simplistic slogans that appeal to racism and paranoia. Like Hitler's brown-shirt fascists of the last century, the NPD's skinheads are marching in the streets, projecting an image of resolute toughness and deliberately invoking the images of the Nazi era. By the late 1990s the government finally mounted a consequential political and legal counterattack.

Of all the fringe right-wing political parties vying for bitter and bigoted supporters in Germany these days, the NPD enjoys the greatest success in recruiting young people to its banner—a flag that looks remarkably like the old Nazi standard, minus the officially banned broken cross, the swastika.

I had the uncomfortable opportunity to meet with the clever, manipulative, mostly middle-aged men who are behind this flag and the movement it represents. In addition to being alongside them for their march through Greifswald, I sat down with them at their party headquarters for a detailed, and at times bizarre, interview and debate.

To the German government's experts who are responsible for tracking political extremists, the connection between the NPD and the wave of brutality perpetrated by skinheads is clear and unmistakable. Government officials no longer have trouble finding the words: "The NPD is using its money and infrastructure to provide cues" to the murderers in the streets while feeding them ideological candy for their vulnerable brains, making them feel as though they are ennobled, worthy knight defenders of a true and pure Germany.

That's why Interior Minister Otto Schily built a strong public case to support the government's request to the Constitutional Court to ban the NPD, the first time since the 1950s that the government identified an existing political party as presenting such a serious threat to the German constitution and democracy itself that it ought to be outlawed. "This is a party that generates violence," Schily announced when he decided to target the NPD. "There is an essential kinship between the Nazis and the NPD." Schily's report to the German parliament cites NPD documents filled with calls for recruiting skinheads as "political soldiers" who will fight a "war on the streets" to restore a Germany for Germans only.

THE NPD HEADQUARTERS building is located in a working-class district of eastern Berlin. The door is a steel plate with no windows. The front of the building is streaked with a mess of red paint thrown by passersby, and spit. A small plaque identifies the tenants. The front windows are covered by drawn shades. I arrive while the NPD staff work to assemble signed petitions from party members and sympathizers who oppose the government's attempt to ban their party. *"Ja zu Deutschland! Nein zum NPD-Verbot!"* read the headlines on the stacks of petitions—Yes to Germany, no to the NPD ban.

One of Chairman Voigt's lieutenants is thirty-seven-year-old Waldemar Maier. This is no unemployed *Ossie* worker from the NPD rank and file. Maier is a political scientist, proud of a degree from Göttingen University. He speaks in a rapid-fire monotone, a style that seems to fit his black turtleneck sweater, black pants, and the decor of the bunker conference room where we talk. The room is festooned with the stark NPD flag and other NPD graphic memorabilia. On one wall hangs a poster featuring a heroic worker in overalls towering in front of a background of factories and industrial smokestacks. The worker is pointing to the NPD name and the legend under it: German workplaces for German workers. Waldemar Maier's title: Special Commissioner to the Chairman of the Party.

Maier is busy when I arrive, assessing the petitions and letters of support for the party and against the effort to ban it. From his point of view, the government's action dates from the widely publicized attack on a synagogue in Düsseldorf. He sees Schily's targeting of the party as a reaction to that attack, and calls his party the real victim. "The actual victim of this attack is the NPD. It triggered the idea of affinities between the Nazi party and the NPD, which is absolutely absurd."

I ask Maier why he thinks so many people, both in Germany and abroad, disagree with him and see the NPD as a Nazi heir.

"The only actual correspondence between both parties," he says, in what may be an attempt at a joke, "is that both start with an 'N.'" He then proceeds to acknowledge the party's use of code words that resonate with Nazi sympathizers, even as he tries to explain that the NPD uses those words innocently. "There are still words like *Volksgemeinschaft* [people's community] that were used in the days of the Nazi party. We use this word too. But it has a different connotation. We have to rebuild the connotation of this word because of changes on the international economic scene."

I suggest that the effect of using such a word just reinforces the belief that the NPD looks to Nazi history for guidance.

He tries again. "It used to have another meaning during the Third Reich," he says about *Volksgemeinschaft*. "But we cannot invent a new language, therefore it is easier to use the old. There are a lot of taboos in German politics. This is one of the reasons it is so difficult for our party." Next he blames the messenger. "Everything is interpreted by the media." And then he goes on to make it clear that he knows how to appeal to his constituency with language. "We strive for the sustainability of human beings, their *Lebensraum*, on German territory." His use of *Lebensraum* is a direct challenge to the mainstream and a wink and a nod to the rank and file.

Look up *Lebensraum* in the dictionary and you find "space to live and develop." But as co-opted by the Nazis, it became the word used to rationalize Germany's territorial usurpations in Austria, Czechoslovakia, Poland, across the Rhine, and beyond.*

---

*That the German language is stuck with the Nazi meaning of the word was made clear to me in a language class in Bonn, when I was first studying German. I constructed the compound out of *Leben* (life) and *Raum* (space) and used it in a sentence to answer a question aloud. There was a noticeable gasp in the classroom from my more experienced peers, and the instructor proceeded to lecture me on the historical context that I had neglected to take into account.

But it's not just terminology, I insist to Waldemar Maier, it's also typography and graphic design. I point to the flag.

Again Maier is brazen in his acknowledgment of the relationship between his work and the Nazi days. "Yes, of course," he readily agrees. "This is all part of our history. We don't want to liberate ourselves from our history. It is longer than twelve years. We regard Hitler like other historical figures." He mentions Bismarck and Martin Luther as examples. "It would be too simple to talk about the 'goodies' and the 'baddies.'"

He resents the carte blanche given to Jews who wish to immigrate and "get admitted just because of their Jewishness." But he favors the fast track for those Soviet-bloc ethnic Germans wishing to start a new life in a Fatherland they never knew. "Well, of course. We want to keep the border open for the brothers and sisters of our people, because they don't have a future in those countries." But he makes his racial, religious, and national preferences clear. "The boat is full. Integration is no longer possible. In many cities there are certain districts in which the proportion of foreign children in kindergartens and schools is higher than 50 percent. As a consequence, the locals move out and we have a ghetto." He says it again, "The boat is full. We want to be friendly," he says about foreign immigrants, including Jews, "but it is better to support them in their home countries."

Maier's boss, Udo Voigt, arrives in the conference room.

Because his words are so contrary to anything remotely resembling American values, I triple-checked the translation of this interview to make certain that I fairly and meticulously represent in English the words of the political leader the German government wants to silence.

"Our party is not against the constitution," he tells me, "so there is no reason to ban it. All the reasons for the ban are unrelated fabrications by the government. They want a multicultural society in Germany, similar to the United States. The NPD, as a nationalist party, is stepping in on behalf of the maintenance of the German race. We are against globalization of big business in Germany, and we support the renationalization of German industries. We wish to make business owners responsible to their race."

Voigt smiles. He's a stocky man, dressed in business clothes, exuding the pained look of the injured party, acting confused about the government's offensive against his organization. I ask him why he believes Interior Minister Schily has moved to ban the NPD. Acutely aware that the German government is building its case to outlaw the party and silence him, Voigt's message to me is cautiously worded.

Udo Voigt

"One could say it is because German youth votes NPD," is his explanation. "In the last state elections we had a high percentage of first-time voters between eighteen and twenty-three years of age. In that category the NPD had more votes than the party in power. That's why they think we are dangerous and want to ban our party. But that is no basis in a democracy for banning a party. That is something you have to live with and something you have to debate."

I turn the talk to NPD policies, particularly the party's position regarding the exodus of Jews to Germany. Voigt had come into the conference room unannounced and unexpected. We are standing as we talk, faces close together. During my experiences in Germany I've found that Americans tend to seek more physical space than Germans during conversations, whether those talks are business or personal. Voigt's face so close to mine is both fascinating and disconcerting. With his neatly clipped

brush moustache, it is impossible not to make mental compar-
isons with Hitler, especially as the moustache jumps with a ner-
vous tic between his answers to my questions.

"These Soviet Jews are turning to us," he laments. "We don't
understand why they come straight to Germany. They have their
country, Israel. We feel they should go to Israel. We think a multiracial state will not work in Germany, that it's the last thing
that would work anywhere in the world. We see, as an example,
what's happening in Bosnia, in Serbia, in the former Yu-
goslavia." Then he addresses me directly. "You, yourself, are
from the States. You know which races there are in the U.S.A.,
what differences and problems there are with Latinos and
blacks, immigrants and nonwhite races. This is a day-to-day
fight. Certain races are contrary. Because of this we are trying to
ensure that Germany stays the land of the Germans. And we
think we should not be punished for having this opinion, nor
should the party be banned."

And what exactly is a German, I wonder aloud. I ask him to
define a German for me. What constitutes this German that Germany should stay the land of, this German threatened by immigration? It's a question that seems especially appropriate in this
blue-collar neighborhood of Berlin, a city built and peopled by
immigrants since its earliest days: Dutch, French Huguenots,
Italians, Poles, Scots, Silesians, Galicians, Saxons, Pomerani-
ans, Prussians, Lithuanians, Russians, and, of course, Jews. So
many of these foreigners filled early Berlin that they took on a
collective nickname: *Rucksack Berliners*. This mix was augmented in more recent years by Turks, Greeks, and Portuguese
on the west side of the Wall, all so-called guest workers. On the
east side the imported workers were Vietnamese, and African
students came to study. Add to this the American, British, and
French occupiers who chose to settle. How often demagogues
fail to realize that they betray their ignorance and prejudices
when they try to explain themselves. Udo Voigt's answer is not

only simplistic; as he traps himself with his words, he becomes farcical.

"A German is someone who was born in Germany," he begins, moustache twitching, "with German parents, is familiar with Germany, speaks the German language, and lives according to German culture. A German, of course, has had German fairy tales told to him during his childhood and has made himself familiar with German stories, and basically all things German—stories of the bad times as well as the good times."

Fairy tales?

I note the history of immigration into Germany and suggest to Voigt that it's too late to prevent Germany from becoming a nation of immigrants.

He rejects the premise, his eyes narrow as he explains why. "Really, it is never too late when one recognizes the possibility of a political turnaround. The fact is that today in Germany we have an almost 10 percent immigrant population here as guests. We have nothing against guests, but guests can also return home. We say it is the job of politics to find ways to send these people who have spread into Germany back to their home countries. On the other hand, we are convinced that in a country of eighty million there will always be foreigners living here, some minimal percentage. But the measurements show that the boat is full. If more foreigners come, murder and violence will be the consequence."

So in Udo Voigt's ideal world, what role is there for foreigners in Germany? His answer is clear: put them on an airplane and get them out of Germany, where they do not belong.

"If you give the German race and German youth no hope, and produce millions of unemployed, this will be a threat to our people. These foreigners live here supported by the government. They are marginalized; almost all of them live in slums. On the one hand, the government wants cheap workers. On the other hand, they don't care for the people they have brought here. These people live in conditions not worth living in. The government's money would be better spent sending these people back to their native countries and financially supporting them so that they might have a future *there*."

The German government has been struggling since reunification to develop eastern Germany. Billions of dollars have poured into the region, rebuilding the devastated infrastructure and retraining the society. But the problems of transition to a market economy have proved much more difficult than forecast. At the same time all of Germany has suffered from the global recession beginning in the late 1990s. As the German economy stagnated, unemployment soared. All these factors played into Udo Voigt's game plan to seduce frustrated Germans to his party's platform, Germans who feel disfranchised and left behind by reunification.

Voigt believes most foreigners in Germany don't want to become Germans, even the Turks who help fuel Germany's economy and have been living in Germany for generations. He grudgingly acknowledges that citizenship could be an alternative, at least in theory, for some immigrants.

"If they are willing to integrate themselves and they are ready to learn the language. But most Turks don't want to learn the language. They don't want to accept German culture and leave their culture behind. Instead they raise their children as Turks, they go to Koranic schools. They are not ready to be dominated by traditional German culture or to compromise with the host nation. They want to weaken a strong state, form a state within a state, and no one can allow that."

Udo Voigt and his National Democratic party watch with satisfaction as the NPD increases its ranks. He credits all the publicity the party has been receiving since the government spotlighted it as a threat as one reason for its growing appeal. He tells me he anticipates the party will survive and will continue successfully to balance the restrictions on absolute free speech in Germany with the party's public and private behavior.

"We handed in our written response to the government's *Ver-*

botantrag [attempt to ban the party as unconstitutional]," he says. "The court will decide whether the case goes forward or not. We have asked to halt the process because we think we have the right to be treated like any other party in Germany."

Voigt reiterates his oft-heard declaration that the NPD is an example of mainstream politics in Germany today. "It is our view that we are a democratically built party like any other party in Germany. We will participate in elections in every state," he insists with confidence. So far, he and the NPD continue to prevail in the courts.

Certainly the surprise showing of immigrant-basher Jean Le Pen in the first round of the 2002 French presidential elections proves that a swing to the scapegoating right wing is not unique to Germany's disgruntled masses. Jörg Haider and his far-right Freedom party enjoyed success at the polls in Austria with a strident anti-immigrant policy. Pia Kjaersgaard, the leader of the far-right Danish People's party, gained votes with the cry, "It's a problem in a Christian country to have too many Muslims." Despite such disturbing trends toward ultranationalism across Europe, when a politician such as Udo Voigt develops a power base in Germany, the concern of Germans and the world is appropriate. Because of Germany's unique history during World War II and the Holocaust, there is no alternative to such special concern when the subjects are Germany and hate.

We say our goodbyes and I make my way out of the NPD headquarters building. As the fortresslike front doors are unlocked for me, an NPD staffer presents me with a packet of colorful giveaways: pens, pins, cigarette lighters, bumper stickers, and the like. Typical political party trifles. They sat on my desk for a few months. At first I thought they would make great gag gifts for colleagues. But the more I looked at them, the more offensive I found the pile of plastic. Somehow the message behind the severe-looking NPD graphics, combined with the mundane medium of modern political trinkets, made these souvenirs particularly onerous. They were not just curiosities based on their uniqueness. Rather, they seemed dangerous because of their bland ordinariness. When I finally threw them in the trash I felt a great sense of relief.

ACCORDING TO surveillance reported by the Office for the Protection of the Constitution, most right-wing German extremists, at least for tactical reasons, say they are against terrorist attacks because they fear that such plans would come to the attention of security authorities and result in increased criminal prosecution. Individual right-wing political activists have called for a violence-oriented strategy for the achievement of political aims.

The Office for the Protection of the Constitution warns that the use of violence as a means for achieving political goals is being encouraged in the lyrics of skinhead music, lyrics rationalized by organizers for the NPD and other political parties, and justified in their neo-Nazi publications and on their Internet sites.

"Heil, comrades!" is the welcome on one such Internet site. Others sell Nazi paraphernalia alongside their tirades against Jews and foreigners. Most of these websites operate from the United States, where the perpetrators are protected by the First Amendment and are safe from the prosecution for hate crimes that would result were they based, or their operators even traveling through, Germany. These cyber soapboxes, along with their magazine and newspaper counterparts, often invoke the threat of violence. The Bulletin for Revolutionary National-Socialists, for example, writes that if its followers "took up armed struggle, they would train their sights on the enemy, and radical action would be taken to get down to the root of the trouble."

Government investigators say that since the early 1990s, when German neo-Nazis began venting their frustrations with unemployment and their hatred of foreigners by using violence, music has played a role in rallying the troops. "Time and again they have entered the picture with spontaneous acts of violence and with their aggressive right-extremist music, which sometimes also incites hatred and violence," according to German government experts analyzing the surging number of illegal right-wing incidents, from terrifying acts of public and private intimidation to murder. These experts say that now, despite more than a hundred murders attributed to these gangs of disaffected young people, the skinheads are much less of a threat than they could easily become. "One reason would seem to be that unstructured, violence-inclined youth lack the leaders" who would be able to initiate or coordinate their activities on a national or even regional basis. No charismatic natural leader has yet risen to prominence among the German right-wingers. Udo Voigt, for all his and the NPD's recruiting successes, comes across more as an irritated and irritating middle-aged businessman than a rousing pied piper.

That organizing gap may be narrowing. "The NPD," reports the Frankfurter *Allgemeine Zeitung*, the conservative nationally circulated daily, "is on tour like a troop of experienced dogcatchers, scooping up alienated and confused young people while teachers complain that they lack the authority even to break up neo-Nazi gatherings in schoolyards." Right-wing organizers have learned how to balance their message of hate with the protections of free speech afforded to Germans by the post–World War II democracy.

Pounding hard in the background of this right-wing extremist ugliness is the white power music of the skinheads. The music is a major organizing tool for the NPD, which sponsors skinhead concerts across Germany. The Office for the Protection of the Constitution reports that while the majority of the bands residing in Germany "refrain from making sound recordings of lyrics containing punishable content [like shouting *Heil Hitler* or denying the truth of the Holocaust], hate-mongering versions of songs with punishable lyrics by well-known bands are quite often played at concerts. During such performances, criminal offenses are frequently committed by members of the audience."

A recording by the band Die Härte,* titled "National Deutsche Welle," is an example of what's being sold on the Internet. The CD combines popular tunes with mostly hate-mongering or anti-Semitic lyrics. The following words are examples of the work of Die Härte:

> It's getting dark; the time for it has come again; there's a meeting of the Ku Klux Klan.
>
> The petrol cans are full; the little niggers from their beds now pull!
>
> Now go and fetch the cross to please the Klan and please their boss.
>
> Let's play bonfire games, and that swine goes up in flames.
>
> A song is sung with a snicker.
>
> How great, hurray, hurray; let's roast a nigger!

There are roughly a thousand websites filled with this kind of white racist bigotry and banned Nazi rhetoric. These sites, operating out of the United States, most with text in the German language, are free to deny the Holocaust and to post Nazi propaganda, acts punishable by up to five years' prison in Germany. They glorify Hitler and the Nazis and fuel the growing neo-Nazi movement in Germany. Authorities in both countries date this phenomenon from the mid-1990s.

German diplomat Walter Leuchs, an expert on the neo-Nazi movement, says his government knows who many of the perpetrators of this hate speech are, but he says catching them is difficult and rare. "The German government, of course, can control such spreading of neo-Nazi material on websites only if the servers are in Germany or the people spreading this material are in Germany. Even foreigners living in other countries and

---

*Die Härte means the hardness, roughness, toughness, harshness, severity.

spreading such material on web servers downloaded in Germany are liable to prosecution in Germany. An Australian-based website official has been sentenced to ten months in a German prison for his support of neo-Nazi activities and propaganda." The German-born Australian citizen Frederick Toben made the mistake of traveling back to Germany, where he was picked up by police who were on the lookout for him. He was convicted of insulting the memory of the dead by denying the Holocaust. Toben complained, "Germany is trying to rule the world again by saying that people who access the Internet have no choice. If someone is offended by the material, they can switch off." But except for anomalies such as the Toben case, the German government concedes there's not much it can do to shut down those websites operating outside its territory.

"They are awful," Walter Leuchs tells me with disgust in describing the neo-Nazi web pages. "What they usually do is to spread the Auschwitz lie, saying that no Jews or only a few Jews were killed during World War II. Sometimes on the websites they actively propagate hatred against foreigners. Some of them say Germany should be for Germans only, and foreigners should be sent back home. Some of them indeed try to imitate the style of the Nazi party of the thirties, just by the characters they use for writing, those traditional German Gothic characters. They are just awful," the diplomat repeats.

German prosecutors say neo-Nazis use cyberspace to post hit lists of their enemies on line. One such list included more than forty names, members of the political party that formerly ruled East Germany. In addition to the names, the list included telephone numbers, addresses, and favorite bars and restaurants. The posting included the sobering instruction to readers, "You know what you have to do." Another site invites postings from readers with the message, "Here you can publish the names of ticks [a slang word for left-wing extremists], darkies, and other rabble who deserve one on the nose." Police take the threats seriously.

"The German government has," says Leuchs, "on different occasions, discussed these neo-Nazi web activities with American authorities. Of course, it's a difficult question. You Americans have your American Constitution and your American law, and we Germans don't have to tell you how to apply this law or tell you which laws you have to have. So there are limits to what can be done." He shakes his head. "It certainly is a problem," he says, because the neo-Nazi sites not only spread hate propaganda, they help neo-Nazis with their activities. "They use the Internet to encourage themselves, to coordinate their interests, and to feel strong and self-confident."

One option considered by the German government is to seek extradition from the United States of website owners and operators who disseminate material accessible to Internet users in Germany. Not a likely scenario, according to U.S. Justice Department spokesman John Russell. "In order to have extradition, you have to have dual criminality in both countries, and this situation doesn't meet that standard." Internet technology allows German-based neo-Nazis to post material on the Internet servers operating in the United States from their homes and offices in Germany.

A sampling of the material on offer includes the text of *Mein Kampf*. (Hitler's book continues to be illegal to sell in Germany, except to journalists and scholars.) The sites in question also offer Nazi memorabilia for sale: military insignia, uniforms, and the like. These sorts of things are also illegal to trade in Germany unless the use serves public awareness, research, education, or art—standards the neo-Nazis, of course, cannot meet. Video games can be accessed, games such as "KZ Manager," a perverse use of the technology that offers players the opportunity to choose who is sent to concentration camp gas chambers. Another bizarre development was initiated on a site operated by Gary Lauck. Lauck served time in a German prison for importing racist literature and now avoids German authorities by staying at home in Nebraska. His technology support staff hacked a game popular in Germany called "Grouse Hunt." The object of "Grouse Hunt" is to shoot pheasants. On Lauck's site, the birds were replaced as targets by Stars of David and yarmulkes. The original game designer was able to force Lauck to remove the doctored game from his web offerings, based on a charge of copyright violation.

19 □ *A Jewish Berliner Discounts the Neo-Nazis*

HELLMUT STERN and his family escaped the Holocaust, getting out of Germany just before *Kristallnacht*. He studied music in Shanghai and played in orchestras in Israel and the United States before deciding that he would make a life for himself in Berlin, despite its history. He became first violinist in the Berlin Philharmonic. Stern's decision to return to Berlin shocked his parents, just as the idea of Jews today seeking sanctuary in Germany is repugnant, or at least ironic, for many people worldwide. Stern is delighted with the new exodus to Berlin and the resurrection of the city's Jewish community. But this Berliner, who escapes the harsh German winter every year to a home in Florida, is outraged by what he considers unnecessary emphasis on the dark side.

At his sun-filled Charlottenburg apartment he retrieves piles of photographs from his files. A little boy in short pants smiling on a tree-shaded Berlin street. A young violinist with colleagues. Family portraits. The professional concert violinist in formal wear. The boy and his father, smiling. The family bundled up against the cold in exile in Shanghai.

"As you undoubtedly know," I start our talk, "plenty of Jews worldwide don't want to buy a Volkswagen or take a tour of Berlin, let alone consider moving here."

"And they hate our guts for having come back here," he interrupts. "Or for having come here—as you say, the exodus to Berlin."

So I ask him to explain why he considers Germany an appropriate place for a Jew to settle. Stern is ready with a practiced reply.

"When I'm in America I grow hoarse from discussions with Americans about this. They say, 'How can you go back?' 'How can you live among the Germans?' They have exactly the same prejudices as others have against the Jews, just the other way around."

What is his response to those perpetual questions?

"My answer is, first of all, do not perpetuate prejudices. Prejudice is one of the great sins, I think, one of the greatest of all. You have to be a little more objective. There have been three, four generations since the war. I cannot possibly condemn all these people, especially the young generation. Not only are they not at fault for the crimes of their forefathers, they are very much against them." He notes the November 9, 2000, demonstration as an example: "Two hundred thousand people on the streets of Berlin demonstrating for human rights and against racism, against anti-Semitism. I have never seen in America a demonstration of such a large number of people against racism, against anti-Semitism."

"Perhaps," I offer, "the very fact that there is a demonstration of this magnitude in Germany today, four generations after the Nazi time, suggests that there's something wrong here, since people find it necessary to get out into the streets to say 'Stop.'"

"Again," Stern says, "I would draw a comparison with America. We're both living in democracies. So why don't the American people get up and demonstrate against what's going on in America? The crime and all that? Even racism. Here if you utter anti-Semitic remarks you will be condemned. Is that the case in America?"

I tell Stern about my chat with the taxi driver who brought me to his Charlottenburg house from the Zoo Station. The driver keeps his radio on whenever he takes a fare into East Berlin so that the dispatcher knows where he is and what's going on inside the cab. He doesn't cruise for fares on the eastern side of the city but drops his passengers and heads directly back to the west. He told me he was afraid on the east side. Stern is again ready with an answer.

"Yeah, the taxi driver in Little Havana or in Liberty City in Florida will tell you the same thing."

"But you're not actually saying that you can draw parallels between American history and the German history?" I ask.

Hellmut Stern

"Definitely not, definitely not. I am just trying, first, to draw your attention to the fact that prejudice is no good, wherever it occurs. We have to fight it. Second, of course we have a small minority—a very, very small minority of young people who are committing violent crimes against foreigners, against Jews. These same people would find victims for their crimes if there weren't a single Jew in Germany, or foreigner, or black person, Chinese, Vietnamese, whatever. They would find another group. It might be bicyclists. In other words, it's the same kind of people who commit hate crimes or road-rage crimes. Only here they acquire from some of the real hardcore neo-Nazis or right extremists a little ideological framework. They are even happy to be called right extremists because their need for violence has been covered over with ideology.

"It's so very difficult to be objective. I grew up here, went to a Jewish school. I lived through all the persecution here. Now I have to tell you something that again will not be favorably received in America. All of us here who were persecuted, we looked at America, we looked at Great Britain, we looked for a place to escape. We didn't have the money. The brutal quota system in America, and in other countries, would not allow us to escape to any of those countries, though the whole world could see how we were being persecuted."

Hellmut Stern and his family tried to leave Germany when Hitler first came to power.

"I was ten years old when we finally left in 1938. My parents made attempts to leave in 1933. My father was a very political-minded person; he knew what was coming. He talked about it all the time. Yet we couldn't leave because we were poor, we had no money. We had nobody in America to give us an affidavit, as it was called in those days. We had no one to support us. The British demanded a thousand pounds sterling for entry into Palestine—a fortune for us. We couldn't even dream of going to Palestine in those days. The French and the Swiss turned us back at the border. It was the Swiss who asked the Nazis to mark our passports so that they would know right away who was a Jew and who was not. We had ordinary German passports, then the Germans stamped the big red 'J' on them. Now, it was ironic that the Japanese, the allies of the Nazis, practically saved our lives. We went to Japan. The Japanese occupied China, which was the last possible escape for us. They allowed us to get to Manchuria. So how do you think I should feel?" He takes a breath. "I never forgot that."

"You never forgot what?" I asked.

"That we could not go to America, which to us was paradise. Roosevelt was our idol. And Roosevelt received all the reports from Germany, by film and by newspapers. Everything was reported to America."

"So your family packed up." I try to encourage him to return to his biography.

"Packed up!" he mocks me and laughs. "Packed up," he laughs again. "Packed up is not the word. We couldn't even pack because there was a Nazi official sitting in our two rooms, watching whatever we put into boxes. We could take nothing except for some personal souvenirs and pictures and whatnot. The Nazis had an official there who packed our things, and we had to show him everything we put in the boxes, and he allowed it or he didn't. He said to my mother, 'Now you can pack some of your valuables.' He couldn't believe it when we said, 'There aren't any.' Because Jews are always rich, Jews own all the money in the world, of course, and here, suddenly, were Jews who didn't."

Stern is talking fast, full of emotion and memory. "Have some juice," I offer. I don't want Stern to lose his voice.

"We had our passports and a valid exit visa." The year was 1938 when they left Germany, the year of *Kristallnacht*. "And of course after that date we were very much afraid that they might not let us out anymore."

Hellmut Stern and his family spent the war years in Manchuria. But the German and Japanese surrenders did not mean they could return to Berlin. "We got stuck in China again because we had the Communists coming in—the Soviet Army first, then the Chinese Red Army. We got stuck there until the end of '49. It wasn't exactly where we wanted to spend our lives. We had been forgotten by the world."

By 1949 young Hellmut Stern was twenty-one years old. He had been living in exile since he was ten.

"There was only one place to go: Israel. Which was fine with us. It took us two months to get to Haifa because we had to go around Africa. The Suez Canal was closed by the Egyptians for ships to Israel." During those long ship passages to China and on to Israel, Stern developed deep resentment against the British government. "They didn't let us off the boat in Bombay or in Hong Kong because we had the 'J' on our passports. Do you realize the irony of that? German passengers who had no 'J' in their passports were allowed to leave the ship, to go to Bombay or Hong Kong. We with the 'J' were turned down by the British. The British recognized the 'J' of the Nazis. The Japanese did not. Think of the irony of that."

But Stern wants to make it clear that his exile was not one of suffering, especially compared with Jews who survived the war in Germany. "We had four categories of persecuted people. The first ones were those in the early 1930s with money and connections, whether in America or somewhere overseas. They could leave and left early. They established a new life for themselves somewhere else, and they were happy ever after. Then there were those who did not have money, who were not being let into other countries, especially the Western democracies, and who had to, as a last resort for refuge, go all the way to China, to Shanghai, or even farther as we did. I belong to that category. Then there was the category of Jews saved right here by some German human beings. I say 'human beings' because the others, I'm afraid, stopped being human. The last category—they were deported and finally murdered." Of the survivors, he believes, those who stayed in Germany and Berlin suffered most. "Their fate and our fate in immigration was absolutely different. What they went through during the Nazi years cannot be compared with what we went through, even though we were pretty badly off in China."

Hellmut Stern remembers his time in Israel with fondness. "In Israel I was quite content. We had no money, but neither did anyone else, except for a few. It was sort of a pioneer spirit there. Almost like the Wild West. People were building their nation. I was lucky to get into the Israel Philharmonic Orchestra. So I played the violin, did my job. Of course I saw a lot and I met many interesting people. But my father couldn't live with the reality of Israel. He was a Zionist really, but his Zionism was an illusion, a utopia. He didn't speak the language; he knew nothing but German. He couldn't adapt to the cultural environment of all those different people in such a small space. I had a sister in America, in Chicago. She said, 'Well, I can't help you while you're there. Come over here.'" He takes another breath before the story of his odyssey circles back to Berlin. "I finally got into American orchestras." Hellmut Stern played five years in America before deciding to return to Europe. "You see," he insists, "in America the social status of an orchestra musician isn't very high. In Israel we enjoyed the greatest respect. We were on the same level with a minister. Oh," he says dreamily, "to be a member of the Israel Philharmonic, that was something. In America it was nothing. There we had short seasons. We had no big salaries, really. You had to be a good musician in order to join all those great orchestras in America, but a musician had nothing to say. In Israel we had a very democratic setup in the orchestra. In America a normal orchestra musician has nothing to say in artistic or organizational matters. He just has to keep his mouth shut, play his fiddle, and go home. So it's very undemocratic in America, really."

After escape to China, settlement in Israel, and finally success in America, a perhaps understandably cynical Hellmut Stern says he looked back longingly at the Old World.

"For me, Europe started with Berlin. I couldn't help that. I had to go first to Berlin because this is my hometown, and I have never forgotten it. Although I was just ten years old when I left, I was always homesick. Many people don't understand that, they even condemn it. My parents don't quite understand it. "How can you . . . ?" He's talking to himself, asking the unfinished question dreamily. "It's a phenomenon, maybe. I don't know. It was there. So I came to Berlin, and of course I had my fiddle with me. I heard there was a vacancy in the orchestra, in the Berlin Philharmonic. And I said, 'Why shouldn't I try?' Because the Berlin Philharmonic was a household word with us."

"Your family," I suggest, "the associates you have had all over the world in the Jewish communities, are saying to you, 'How can you go to Berlin?' This is where the Holocaust started, and this city is populated by the people who were the murderers. What was going on that attracted you back here?"

"I agree with you that the murderers were still among us," says Stern about his return in the early sixties. "On the other hand, a new generation was already coming up. The Americans offered democracy to the Germans on a silver plate. The Germans took it. They established a real democratic state. No doubt about it. Of course, many people don't want to acknowledge that. But this is the truth. We have seen it again during the [November 9, 2000] demonstrations." But Stern was not just homesick. He was professionally motivated. "Don't forget, please, I wasn't only a Jew, I was also an orchestra musician. I know of many musicians who would be happy to get into the Berlin Philharmonic Orchestra because it is the top, absolute top."

"But what about living in a city that had been purged of Jews, and coming back at that time, when people were saying to you, 'Don't go there.'"

Stern says the fact that so many countries refused him asylum when he fled Germany made it easier for him to return. "I can never be apologetic about the crimes of the Germans, but [the countries that refused refuge] were supporters of those crimes, even if they didn't think so. In my mind, all the Western countries collaborated with the Nazis simply by standing there watching, not doing anything, turning their eyes away. I didn't feel that bad coming to the country that committed the crimes in the first place. That sounds very bitter," he says, "but that's how it was."

Hellmut Stern returned to his hometown Berlin after an absence of twenty-three years, arriving August 12, 1961. His timing for experiencing history is amazing. "On the 13th of August I was standing at the Brandenburg Gate, watching as the Communists were closing it, building the Wall. It wasn't a wall yet, it was wire at that time. I was right on time, as you said." He laughs.

"You ask how I could come here? At that time, don't forget, Germany was the closest ally of America. When the Wall was finally built, Berlin, West Berlin, was an object of admiration for the whole world, an object to be saved if necessary. Now if Germany and Berlin had become the closest ally of the West, why shouldn't I come here? Why should I think differently from Kennedy?"

"I understand what you're saying intellectually, but from an emotional point of view I find it . . ." Stern cuts me off and mocks my continuing questions about why he returned.

"I'm afraid that prejudice, especially in America, is so great that in your minds Germany was and is still roamed by Nazis, shouting anti-Semitic slogans. This is bull, you know? This is not right. I'm not afraid to walk in the streets. As a matter of fact, I even went to a so-called right-extremist youth club. And you know why I went? Discussions. Analysis. Why is there violence in the state of Brandenburg? Who is doing something about it? I decided that those fourteen-, fifteen-, and sixteen-year-old kids are anti-Semitic without ever having seen a Jew. I decided to show them one. I went to them. People admired my great courage. That's no courage whatsoever. I came to them, I said, 'You know, guys, I don't think you're so bad. You're just listening to the wrong people. And I came here to show you a Jew. That's all. I'm not a journalist. I'm not a photographer.'"

Hellmut Stern, the concert violinist, the childhood exile, the returned German Jew, then recounts for me in detail his intriguing and productive time with Brandenburg skinheads.

"I said to them, 'I came here to show you a Jew.' One of them said, 'Ah, come on, you're not a Jew, you're one of us.' I was really astonished when he said that. I said, in Berlin slang—they speak Berlin slang, and to be on the same level I spoke it too—I said, 'Sure, I'm one of you, but I'm also a Jew. You know there is this phenomenon, the German Jew.' They said, 'How can you be a German and a Jew?'

"I tried to explain that. I said to them, 'You see, you have been misled by people who want to use you, they want to manipulate you, because you don't know any of these things. You know nothing of German history. You know nothing of Jewish

history or what Jews are. What is Jewishness? You have no idea.'
They were quite interested and asked, 'So what do you believe
in?' Unfortunately I had a hard time answering, because my
faith isn't that strong. While I consider myself a Jew, I'm not one
of those highly religious Jews, to put it mildly. I said, 'You know,
Jews are not just a religious group, they are also a nation in a
way.' Then I started to tell them how two thousand years ago we
lost the state and how we were thrown out and lived in all the
countries and became members of those societies, became subjects of those societies, and then in Germany at a certain time
we were welcomed together with other foreigners who may even
have been your forefathers. They may have been Huguenots,
they may have been Poles—many names here are actually Slavic
or Polish, Czech or whatever, Russian. 'So you don't even know,'
I said, 'that it's the foreigners who made up German culture, especially of this city. And the Jews were the most ardent Germans
of all. We were Germans of Mosaic confession, as we used to
say.'

"That's how I grew up. It was never a question. I was a German just like I breathed the air of Berlin. I told them a little bit
about that, and I tried to tell them how many Jews participated
in the first war, how many Nobel Prize winners there are among
the Jews, about the musicians and doctors and scientists. I gave
them that whole big speech, you know?

"They listened very attentively. Then came the crucial question. 'But why have you been persecuted all this time?' Again I
had to go back two thousand years and tell them that the Jews
were also good scapegoats. They understood that because they
feel themselves to be scapegoats. Many of them come from broken families, horrible social situations. No future. No perspective. No work—not everyone, but many have no work. The kids
were very attentive, very interested.

"My achievement, I think, is that the next time one of those
manipulators comes to talk to them, some of them will remem-

ber me when he talks about the Jews, and they will say, 'Now wait a minute, that guy was a Jew. He wasn't at all like what you are saying.' At least they will start thinking."

I try to bring Stern back to the escalating violence against Jews and foreigners in Germany, the murders, assaults, fire-bombings, and desecrations. "It's not as if there are no problems with right-wing violence in Germany," I say.

"I see that too," he agrees. "But it has been so overblown. Blown up absolutely out of proportion." His voice is rising, and he's waving his hands in protest. "I'm trying to keep a perspective. Because if a little kid of thirteen rides his bicycle by a syna-gogue with his pals, and he wants to show his courage, and he has a stone in his hand and throws it and runs away, the whole world learns about it. It's as though the greatest event has oc-curred. But this kid is the proudest guy in the world. Next day when he reads about it in the paper, the whole world is paying attention to the little stone he threw. He throws them at churches too. They have been smearing things on Christian cemeteries just as well. Now they know where they can hit back at a society that has neglected them, those little kids. They know that if they paint a swastika somewhere, the whole world will say 'Look at Germany, look at the Nazis there. Isn't it horrible?' But how many swastikas have I seen in America?" Again his voice rises with emotion as he works to prove that Germany is no different than the rest of the world. "How many times have I heard about the kikes? How about that? And nothing happens. No one stands up, and the whole world doesn't find out about it."

I suggest that Nazi history mandates that standards are dif-ferent in Germany. "Wait a minute," he protests. "There is now, as I said, the fourth generation here. These people, the German people, are in general now a decent people, a democratic society. You can't possibly make them accountable for the small minor-ity of stone throwers and—which I don't minimize—the few hardcore Nazis."

And he points out the open immigration policies that Germany has instituted for Jews.

"If you take all those Jewish refugees who are coming to Germany, from Russia especially, they are receiving privileges here that no one knows about. In America no one would get these privileges. Nowhere but in Germany, and these are not German Jews, they are people who were born after the war. They have never seen a German. Just because they're Jews, they're being let in here and they're getting social support that even Germans don't get. This is done by the government. Why isn't that being mentioned at all?"

"That's why I'm writing this book," I remind him.

Obviously Hellmut Stern believes there is a future for the Jewish community in Germany.

"I consider it not only a right, I consider it a necessity that Jewish life be reestablished in this country as a victory over those murderers. They are dead and gone. We're here. This for me is a triumph. And I must tell you something: I personally have never encountered anti-Semitism. I read about it in the paper. I see it on television. I hear it from others. Maybe I'm lucky."

"Between 1961 and today you've never encountered anti-Semitism in Germany?" I ask, incredulous.

"Personally? Nothing. Whether you believe it or not, that's the case. Of course I must admit that I work among a circle of people who would never allow such things. As a matter of fact, the Berlin Philharmonic has several Jews in the orchestra. But I have experienced anti-Semitism in America, yes, in orchestras there definitely."

Hellmut Stern is proud of the exodus to Berlin, pleased that Germany so many years and generations after the Holocaust still feels an obligation to welcome Jewish immigrants. He's convinced the influx makes Berlin a more vibrant city.

"It was always good. How did Berlin grow from a tiny village of fishermen into one of the world's leading cultural centers? Because of all its varied cultures. Just like in America. Germany after the war has moved in this same direction, but some people don't want to recognize that this is a country of immigrants."

20 ☐ *The Weary Nazi-chasing Cop*

THE RISE OF the violent right in Germany is an ongoing nightmare for its individual victims. An example is the 1999 case of twenty-eight-year-old Omar Ben Noui (also known as Farid Guendoul), an asylum seeker from Algeria, living legally in Guben, a little town on the Polish-German border. Guben is just a few miles northeast of Peitz on Highway 97, a rural two-lane blacktop that connects the depressed burgs of far eastern Germany. The southern outskirts of old Guben are defaced by blocks of anonymous-looking apartments which the Communist East German government left littering the countryside. These are urban planning disasters, row after row of poorly constructed eyesores, cosmetically touched up after unification—concrete housing monoliths surrounded by parking lots and faded attempts at landscaping. Populated by so many of the undereducated and unemployed left behind by society after German reunification, these mistakes are ideal breeding grounds for neo-Nazis. Just how severe unemployment is in eastern Germany, especially for younger workers, was made clear by a teacher at a vocational school in Krassow, who announced sadly, "Ninety percent of pupils who leave my school go straight on the dole."

In the Guben sprawl, chased by a mob of right-wing extremists, Omar Ben Noui ran into one of the apartment buildings seeking safety. Instead of finding sanctuary, he smashed into a glass door and bled to death from a severed artery. Guben city officials installed a memorial to the victim near the site of his death.

The simple stone marker is difficult to find. It's affixed to a boulder at ground level, surrounded by worn grass, alone between the parking lot and the sidewalk. Perhaps it is a fitting reminder of Guben's ongoing problems with the violent far right that the memorial looks so alone, reflecting the aloneness of Omar Ben Noui as he met his demise. The inscription is stark. Along with a Christian cross, it states the victim's name and age and the date he—as it says on the marker—*verblutet*. The word in German sounds as harsh as its meaning: bled to death. "Remember," intones the inscription, "oppose racism, oppose violence, oppose xenophobia." The last line on the marker is a quote from the German Basic Law, the constitution: "The dignity of man is inviolable." When I visited the site it was cleaned of recent racist markings. The perpetrators of these types of hate crimes have no difficulty finding the stone; it had been desecrated and cleaned at least seven times in the year before my visit.

By the year 2000 eleven juvenile Guben residents were convicted of charges connected with the assaults on Omar Ben Noui and a friend of his who escaped injury. Only three went to prison; the others enjoyed some sort of probation. One of those convicted, identified by the German police and courts only as nineteen-year-old David B., was found guilty of causing serious bodily injury, vandalism, and duress. His sentence for his participation in the murder: two hundred hours of community service and a warning to stop his violent anti-social behavior.

Before the year was out, David B. was back in police custody, this time charged with being part of a gang that attacked a man whose looks attracted them because his mother was Asian. Arresting officers told reporters that David B. and his cronies yelled anti-foreigner insults at the man and then stabbed him.

That David B. was a repeat violent offender who evaded

prison riled prosecutors and the press. The Brandenburg justice minister responded with a call for severe penalties for the perpetrators of hate crimes, including juveniles such as David B. The national tabloid newspaper *Bild* directed its editorial about the case to the sentencing judge, demanding, "How much understanding can the brutal Nazi David B. expect from you this time?"

Note that the paper did not use the modifier "neo" when calling David B. a Nazi. It reminded me of a chat I had with a friend after I moved into a flat in Berlin and learned that my apartment building was one of many owned by the Munich publisher and politician Gerhard Frey. An example of Frey's newspapers' content can be best summed up by the headline in his *Deutschland Wochen-Zeitung* weekly just after the Berlin Wall fell: *Deutschland, Deutschland über alles, über alles in der Welt.* Another of his newspapers is the *Deutsche National Zeitung.* Its typography evokes the look of Nazi propaganda in much the same manner as the material passed around by the NPD. A harsh cross fits neatly between *National* and *Zeitung* on the paper's masthead.

"Is Frey a neo-Nazi?" I asked my German colleague after I saw his publications.

"No," was the answer, "he's an old Nazi."

Perhaps no distinction ought be drawn between those followers of the Nazis in the thirties and forties and those who engage in similar acts today. I use the term neo-Nazi in this book simply to identify those such as David B. who are contemporary examples.

After looking at the anonymous doorway where Omar Ben Noui died, I drive on into the center of Guben, a place that looks pleasant enough, a typical small eastern German city, filled with bustling shops. I stop at a Turkish *Imbiss* for a falafel. Two Turks are behind the counter. It's just before noon and lunchtime, and the place is empty. So we chat as I eat standing at one of the chest-high tables favored by Germans seeking a quick bite. Without hesitation, once they learn of my work as a journalist, they start telling of the prejudice and discrimination they feel as Turks in Germany. "We always fear danger is near," they say. "We keep a low profile and don't say anything controversial." As local patrons begin to come into the shop for a sandwich, the Turks stop talking politics with me and speak politely to the customers while preparing the food. Once the door closes and we're alone again, the stories spew forth once more, stories they do not want their German neighbors to hear them tell.

Another example of a victim is Volkan Erkurt. Born in Berlin of Turkish parents, Erkurt was chased out of a disco on the east side of Berlin by a group of foreigner-haters who caught up with him, stomped him with their steel-tipped boots, and carved a swastika and the word "death" on his head with a pocketknife. "It's been like this since the Wall fell," said Erkurt, "bad news for anyone who is not German."

Not violent, but certainly disconcerting, was the response of an angry crowd during a ceremony to rename a Berlin street Jüdenstrasse—Jews Street. The Nazis had changed the name to Kinkelstrasse when they controlled the city. The trouble occurred in November 2002, just two years after Berlin streets filled with the marchers calling for tolerance. Berlin Jewish leader Alexander Brenner was making a speech praising the return of the street's former name. Demonstrators began shouting, "*Jüden raus!*" and "Jews have no God!" and "Jews are to blame for everything!" They booed. Brenner quit his prepared speech and addressed the hecklers directly, saying, "You are putting yourselves in the same category as neo-Nazis." Germany's elected Jewish leader, Paul Spiegel, was incensed, saying the disruptions were "further proof that inhibitions about anti-Semitic sentiments are falling if ordinary people start shouting slogans such as '*Jüden raus*' in public." Spiegel was particularly concerned about the public nature of the insults, which he placed in historical perspective. "Germany hasn't seen anything like this since 1945." Spiegel regarded the Spandau neighborhood controversy over Jüdenstrasse as an example of the increasing hostility he's witnessed to the exodus to Berlin of Jews from Eastern Europe. "What frightens me most is the large number of those who are indifferent. They have nothing against Jews. But they lack the courage to take a stand against the rabble-rousers."

He could have been describing Klaus-Jüregen Kühl, who runs a bar called Roby's Bistro on what used to be Kinkelstrasse. "I can understand why people are angry," he told reporters after Alexander Brenner was insulted, then insisted, "I don't really care what the street name is. But look at all the costs for new stationery and business cards."

IN RESPONSE TO escalating right-wing violence near Berlin in Brandenburg, the state government allocated increasing resources to police charged with curbing neo-Nazi crimes. Heiner Wegesin is the chief of police intelligence for Brandenburg. I met with him at the Forum Hotel on Alexanderplatz in Berlin after driving back through eastern Germany from Greifswald following the NPD march. My mind was still full of images of the contorted faces of neo-Nazis chanting their slogans, of the lines of riot police separating the demonstrators and the counterdemonstrators, of the old woman yelling, *"Nazis raus!"*

Wegesin looks more like a businessman than the tough cop he is. He wears a conservative business suit. He keeps his hair short on his balding head. If he wore high-laced boots, jeans, a leather jacket, and a snarl instead of his usually relaxed smile, he could be mistaken for one of the skinheads he's trying to put out of business. Those skinheads, he tells me, attack anyone who looks different from what they perceive a German ought to look like, and in many cases their parents encourage their behavior. "In some regions of Brandenburg," says Wegesin, explaining his working theory of what stimulates recruitment by the NPD and other neo-Nazi groups, "unemployment is 50 percent. We're talking about fifty years of Communist dictatorship and twelve years of Nazi dictatorship before that, no intercultural experience whatsoever—and that's basically the root of our right-wing extremism."

German government officials such as Wegesin, responsible for tracking the rapid rise of the neo-Nazi movement, keep the fact firmly in their minds that when Adolf Hitler was beginning his journey to absolute power back in the 1920s, he and his band of beer-hall bullies were widely dismissed by educated and intelligent people as just another idiot with bad manners, not worthy of much attention and certainly not worthy of concern. While it is true that the rich and powerful Germany of today bears little resemblance to the poor and weak nation that Hitler and his Nazis rallied into a machine of racist hatred, mass murder, and global war, even a few neo-Nazi skinheads committed to violence right now could do terrible damage to individuals and institutions, and threaten German democracy itself.

According to the research of the Office for the Protection of the Constitution, the number of neo-Nazi skinheads and other violence-inclined right-wing extremists in Germany climbed during the 1990s at the rate of about a thousand a year, with the total at the end of the decade estimated by the government at about ten thousand. This number includes both violent offenders and individuals who display a positive attitude toward the use of violence and therefore are taken quite seriously by government investigators as dangerous. Government estimates of Germans who embrace a neo-Nazi philosophy but who distance themselves from violence add up to tens of thousands. For several years police have suspected that weapons and explosives are being acquired and stashed by elements of the right-extremist scene in Germany.

It is this milieu that Wegesin and his agents try to infiltrate and disband. "We basically cover all forms of political extremism as well as doing other classical intelligence work, counterintelligence, and so forth. But of course we invest, I'd say, nearly 80 percent of our resources right now in right-wing extremism."

Wegesin and his agents investigate individuals suspected of violent abuses, and they go after their organizations. "We are talking about having one banned through the Constitutional Court right now, the National Democratic party, the NPD. The NPD is trying to boost the ongoing militant scene." Wegesin sees the NPD and its ilk as criminally dangerous, not as a political threat. "These parties don't have any chance of getting elected into any kind of parliamentary body. We have the so-called 5 percent clause: you need 5 percent of the votes on any level—local, state, federal—to win a seat in parliament. They never get beyond 1 percent."

But he does worry about violence instigated by the rhetoric spewing from the NPD. "What's really dangerous is that we have an unorganized, unstructured militant scene. Basically we're talking about a juvenile gang problem. We're talking about the skinhead movement, and we're talking about a really deep-rooted xenophobia, especially here in eastern Germany. Hopefully it won't become part of the political mainstream, but it provides a seedbed for political extremism." Even after years of studying the delinquents, Wegesin is amazed by their ignorance. "It might not even be a foreigner they attack, just strange-looking German citizens."

These intimidating gangs of juvenile street criminals are not rebelling against their parents. On the contrary. "Obviously the parents' generation, in some cases, encourages this." Wegesin is exhausted by how pervasive the rot is throughout the former East German society. "We are talking about a deep-rooted social problem where people consider themselves underdogs. We're talking about extraordinary unemployment rates. The official rates are around 25 percent. In our social welfare system, no one ends up in the gutter, but in some regions of Brandenburg nearly half the working population has no job." He knows that police work alone is not a cure to what ails Germany. "What do you do? We are talking about a social problem."

A dozen years after German reunification, there are still no signs of substantial improvement in their standard of living for most workers in the former East Germany, workers who often face conditions more difficult than they experienced during the days of Communist dictatorship. One in seven Germans from the east side of the country has responded by moving west; population continues to drop in the East. The region lost almost two million of its citizens in the years between the fall of the Wall in 1989 and the turn of the century—about 10 percent of its population. Wrecking balls and bulldozers claim a growing number of vacant Soviet-era housing blocks. "There's no chance to earn a decent living," one economic refugee from the Baltic Sea port city of Rostock told the *New York Times*. "The only alternatives," said Susanne Kophal about her decision to leave, "are the two classic examples: becoming a taxi driver or working at McDonald's."

As Heiner Wegesin recounts the degenerating realities facing Brandenburg and Germany, his face contorts with expressions of visceral disgust. We're talking in the lobby of the Forum Hotel. When I first visited this place it was owned and operated by the East German government. Built in the seventies in an attempt to convince the world that East Berlin could compete with the flash and glitz of the West, the Forum is burdened with small rooms, low ceilings, narrow corridors, and other architectural deficits that the Intercontinental chain couldn't correct when it took over the hotel and refurbished it to Western first-class standards. But the lobby gleams, and Wegesin's sorry litany of the perdition plaguing Brandenburg and the other new German states seems out of place amidst the calm of the remade Forum.

Wegesin understands there is no quick fix. "Would we really solve problems by having the NPD banned? From an investigator's point of view, if they're banned we can attack their structure, we can dismantle their support of the militant scene, we can seize their funds, and so forth. So if we can do it within our constitutional framework, let's do it. But as I said, the problems are much more deep-rooted."

I tell Wegesin of my meeting at NPD headquarters with party leader Udo Voigt, about Voigt's tirade against foreigners in Germany. Wegesin says there is a direct line from NPD propaganda and speeches to attacks on immigrants and their institutions. He says the thugs in the street get their cues from the likes of the NPD.

"The direct line is that the NPD has the resources. They have money. They have local party chapters. They sponsor skinhead concerts. Skinhead music carries the propaganda message. So the NPD provides the framework. They say the youngsters, especially the skinheads, are the party's political soldiers, fostering their cause, attacking the evil forces that undermine and threaten Germany—foreigners taking away jobs, asylum seekers coming in and being fed. All this nonsense." Wegesin agrees with investigative reporter Frank Jansen that these cadres of troublemakers are not filled with drunks and unemployed. "Most of them have a job, 80 percent of them are not unemployed."

Heiner Wegesin

Despite the successes of the NPD in drawing new members, and the attention of the media and the government, Wegesin's investigations reveal a fractured neo-Nazi movement. "You don't have central control. Different facets cooperate, but they aren't connected in any networking fashion. If there were central control, as intelligence officers, we would prefer it. We could attack it and just take it out, bag those people and that'd be it." Instead, investigators are forced to follow up leads sending them to autonomous groups that link with others informally. "You have the street-gang scene in small cities and villages and very remote rural areas in Germany, where there is nothing to do. You have the old man in the pub waiting for those guys, trying to influence them. You have simply militant people, really not part of the hardcore skinhead scene, taking up Nazi propaganda." Wegesin's concern is that these various components of the current troubles could coalesce into a mass movement. "This propaganda, this right-wing extremism, might become part of the daily mainstream of our culture in some regions and in some age groups. That's the deep-rooted danger."

But he's optimistic that his work can prevent such growth. "I'm not seeing that yet. I think we're still in a phase where things can be turned around. Turnaround will take a few years. It's not just a matter of a tough crackdown by police. That won't work."

What will work?

"Educational programs in schools," he says without hesitation. "A really wide-ranging social effort."

Meanwhile Wegesin orders his officers to hold the line and protect the citizenry.

"Crack down as hard as you can," is his method. It's not always easy, and he's frustrated when he sees the procedures his colleagues in America use. "In Germany we have a different approach to police work. We have a different penal code. Zero tolerance, neighborhood policing, and other approaches that we know have reduced crime in the United States are hard to utilize here in Germany. If you have an apartment and a job, and you assault someone in the street, you won't go to jail in Germany unless you are trying to flee or trying to falsify evidence."

I tell Wegesin about the Turkish restaurant owners I spoke with during lunch in Guben, who lamented the revolving door of Germany's criminal justice system. They told me stories of skinheads arrested and convicted of crimes against foreigners, yet quickly released back into the community, only to be arrested again for the same types of crimes.

"That's correct," he agrees, with refreshing candor for a high government official, saying the German justice system encourages skinhead thugs to repeat acts of violence against the innocent. "And the phrase 'revolving door' really is correct. Of course we can, even within our legal framework, do more. We have to do something before these people drift off into terrorism." Wegesin knows the problems in Guben well. "We are talking about thirty to forty mostly juvenile militants there." And as the Turkish shop owners pointed out, the identities of the delinquents are well known. Wegesin says that under such circumstances, the community must exert peer pressure. "You simply step on the toes of these young people. Everyone who's been a delinquent, who is on the verge of delinquency, must be confronted by the entire community. By the police if necessary, but also by the churches, the unions, and especially by the people responsible for their education. You have to talk to parents as well. You simply have to attack these problems person by person by person."

Wegesin seems exasperated even as he ticks off the constructive plans he hopes will rehabilitate the criminals his department chases. "As a police officer, you must be frustrated," I suggest. "You must want to crack some heads and throw some guys in the backs of squad cars for a trip downtown."

"That's right," he readily agrees. "We don't infiltrate youth gangs of fourteen- or fifteen-year-olds. Within our legal framework we start at the age of sixteen." Reality proves that's often too late. Just a few weeks before we meet, Wegesin tells me, two drunk thirteen-year-old boys were picked up in Brandenburg for assaulting another just because his mother was from Mongolia. While the police are restricted from investigating the activities of young teenagers, right-wing organizations are enticing them. "The skinhead music scene is commercializing and professionalizing tremendously."

I ask Wegesin if he figures these juveniles are just drunk kids in trouble or if they're motivated by ideology. He makes it clear that it's impossible to make such a simple choice. "Their parents are a loser generation in their eyes." Many middle-aged East German workers felt lost after reunification. Even if the factory or store where they worked wasn't shuttered, even if they didn't lose their jobs, they lost their nation and the set of beliefs it foisted on them. "They were dreaming of Marx and Lenin just ten years ago," Wegesin says, "and what does the country look like now?" Much of what's closed down and broken was created during the Nazi and Communist years. What's new and glistening—like the slick Forum Hotel lobby bar—is often out of reach for impoverished eastern Germans, and is imported from the western side. "If you really break it down, it's pure xenophobia," Wegesin says about the origin of the crisis. "It's a deep-rooted feeling of being the underdog, being second class—foreigners, asylum seekers, and Jews are taking away your natural resources. It's a retreat to the primitive conspiracy theories at the root of Nazism and fascism, such as world capital dominated by the Jews, Jews sending in foreign workers." The victims end up being "refugees like this poor guy from Algeria who was killed in Guben, while someone behind the scenes manipulates everything. People with no intercultural experience and education go for these primitive theories."

Heiner Wegesin commands a troop of police specialists who patrol Brandenburg and keep him in touch with day-to-day abuses. "I have a pretty dedicated young crew, and when they drive around the countryside, some of them being hard-core bikers on their Harleys, they come back and say, 'Hey boss, we have to do something. Driving through those villages, you can see people just marching around there, skinheads showing Nazi propaganda, and no one's doing anything about it. They're ruling the village. Hey, let's do something about it.' That gets my blood up."

In some remote villages the skinheads taunt the police, raising the Third Reich salute and chanting, *"Sieg Heil!"*—both activities illegal under Germany's laws restricting speech that endorses Nazi ideas.

Although Wegesin's unit doesn't field enough officers to respond to each neo-Nazi offense, he's convinced the skinheads are on the run. "I think we can get things done. We're not afraid to tackle problems." But he uses the words "shame" and "rage" again as he talks about the lawbreakers. "If you break it down to the individual, it makes you shudder."

I recount to Wegesin my experiences with the Rojsenblat family in Peitz, so hopeful as they made the transition from Ukraine to Germany. "Did they make a mistake?" I ask him. "How dangerous is their new life?"

"I think they may have a security problem that is no graver than yours, walking around as an ordinary citizen in the jungle of Berlin," he says. "But we have to protect these people. We have to look after them. We have to make them aware of the danger and give them a feeling that we're cracking down on these problems."

I ask him what he would have advised if the Rojsenblats had called him before making their decision to emigrate to Germany. "What would you have said to them?" I ask Wegesin. "What do you say to others in that position?"

"Come to Germany," he says without hesitation, "because if you stop coming to Germany, those people who are a shame for our country win. We don't want this again. The vast majority doesn't want this again. If you stop coming, those people will be getting returns on their ugly investment. So please come. We will look after you and will do everything to guarantee your security. I think we can do our job." He reiterates that the police cannot do all that's necessary. Ordinary citizens must take some responsibility for preventing lawlessness. They must engage in what the Germans refer to as "civil courage."

"Civil courage. Let's demand that. Citizens have to practice it. Police can do a lot. You can dismantle certain structures, you can crack down on people. But we need daily civil courage wherever violations of human dignity occur. Even in cases of only verbal abuse, someone has to stand up and say, 'Hey look, we've heard this before. Do you really know what you're talking about?' Teachers have to do this. Churches have to do this."

"Civil courage can be dangerous," I say, reminding him of the rabbi who was punched on the subway for intervening when a subway driver was harassed. "He got a black eye for his trouble."

At least call the police, Wegesin urges. "You can start off by doing that. You don't have to take body combat courses. You don't have to knock anyone down. When two or three young thugs are attacking a rabbi, if five people stand up, the thugs will stop. We've seen that happen. They aren't so courageous. Civil courage is what's really lacking."

21 □ *Song and Dance*

IT SEEMS CLEAR that most Germans treasure basic democratic
virtues and values. Most work hard to try to compensate for the
Holocaust and create a new history for their country. Integration between the Jewish community and the rest of the population is ongoing and often vigorous.

The Jüdisches Gemeindehaus, the Jewish community center,
on Fasanenstrasse, just off the Kurfürstendamm, is headquarters for Berlin's Jewish community. It's built on the site of a
synagogue burned by the Nazis on *Kristallnacht*. The debris lan-
guished through the mid-1950s at the site, and some of it was
used to grace the otherwise drab new building. Berlin police
with machine guns patrol the entrances twenty-four hours a day,
as they do at other Berlin Jewish institutions. Israeli military-
trained volunteer private guards augment the uniformed officers. Their tedious job, standing around waiting for dreaded
possibilities, adds a further grim and onerous tone to the scene
out front, a grey vista augmented by the cityscape: the adjacent
elevated railroad, the gated parking lot, the reminder of the past
presented by the pieces of the old synagogue adorning the new
building. A meal at the kosher restaurant inside or a visit to a
show requires an airportlike trip through security. Bags are
x-rayed and searched, diners and all others must pass through a
metal detector. Guards inside keep watch over a huge array of
security-camera monitors tracking movement in and around the
building.

A typical evening's entertainment at the community center

includes performances such as one I caught of a pulsating Italian Klezmer group. The hall was packed and the wine was flowing as the group was introduced, part of Jewish Culture Days—fourteen days each year celebrating Jewish cultural events throughout Berlin. Andreas Nachama was in the audience and took a bow in recognition of his continuing work reconstructing a strong Jewish presence in Berlin. Smiling, his pixieish eyes bright, Nachama was obviously pleased. This was a delightful piece of his political work, making a speech about the pleasure of participating in an evening of Jewish music.

The band took the stage: a flute, a clarinet, an accordion, a guitar, a string bass, and a violin. The violinist with long stringy hair hanging down from his bald spot and a beard down to his belly looked like one of the stereotypical *Ostjuden* so many Berliners have worried about through the centuries. Tapping his foot and grinning, his looks added an extra dazzle to the stage. The singer, in a beret, stood at stage center filling the hall with exuberant counterpoints to the trills of the clarinet.

DOWN THE ORANIENBURGERSTRASSE from the New Synagogue, at the Hackesche Höfe Theatre, director Burkhardt Seidemann says his company's productions are designed to draw audiences into the Jewish experience. The theatre specializes in Jewish-themed plays and Klezmer music concerts. We sit on his stage together before an evening performance and talk about the role Jewish music and theatre play in changing Berlin. I ask Seidemann if it's possible to rebuild the Jewish community there. "That can't simply be answered yes," he says emphatically. "I say yes, there *must* be a Jewish community in Berlin. That's the decision. Not because it's easy, but because it's important. It's important for Germany."

Burkhardt Seidemann is an intense speaker. Sporting several days' growth of beard, long and flying hair where he's not balding, wire-rim glasses, and a tweedy sports coat, he's another who looks like an *Acht-und-sechziger*, a social activist from the sixties generation. Of course, rebuilding the Jewish community is important for the Jews in Germany, "but I say for *Germany* it is very, very important that there are Jews here again, and that Jews don't live secret lives but live completely in the open." Our meeting on the stage is lit by the theatre's spotlights. Seidemann gestures toward them and says, "Like in this theatre where we sit: under lights." He laughs. He calls his theatre a symbolic place for Berlin's Jews, "where Jews say publicly, 'We're here, and we're going to present our culture.' That, this country needs."

Why is it so important to reestablish Jews and Jewish culture in Germany? I ask. Everyone knows the history, Seidemann reminds me. "Here in Berlin it was planned, the so-called Final Solution of the Jewish Question." He writes these critical words in the air with a finger. "That can't be separated from Germany. We can't just say, 'That has nothing to do with me, sorry.' We can't remake the past, but we can say that we want Jews to live here now. That's resistance against barbarism. That's a decision for mankind, not just for Jews, and not just for Germany."

The surge of skinhead and neo-Nazi violence against Jews is fueled in part by attention, Seidemann says, his analysis enhanced by his theatrical experience. "They live for the publicity they get." The Hackesche Höfe Theatre has been defaced by swastikas scrawled on the outside walls. "When that happens, we don't call journalists because that's what they want, publicity." He looks disgusted. "We clean it off. It is a problem, it must be taken seriously. But these people provoke something else: a stronger resistance," he points to his heart, "and people say, 'Never again.'"

Seidemann refuses to blame youthful rebellion and unemployment for the reactionary right-wing activities, saying there are more dangerous players. "I've traveled often in Eastern Europe where there are political parties with anti-Semitic programs." The propaganda spouting this ideology fuels latent and not so latent anti-Semitism in Germany. But Seidemann opposes making parties in Germany such as the NPD illegal, agreeing that they're likely to prosper underground. "I believe if it's forbidden, many people will find it more attractive. It will take on a mystical air. If the party is out in public, it can be watched."

His theatre's work has diametrically opposed aims. "We are a place where Jews and Germans, consciously and with a goal, get together. That's something new." Burkhardt Seidemann says he starts each Yiddish-language show by speaking to the audience in German about Jewish life. He wants them to understand what he considers a critical aspect of German history and the point of his theatre's work: "There is no German culture without the Jewish element. And there will be no German culture without the Jewish element." Seidemann speaks with his hands flying, and he keeps pointing to his heart when he explains how he sees his audiences responding: coming alive during the performances and leaving with a new feeling in their hearts. It sounds like hyperbole, but I witness it myself later that evening.

While appreciating his successes, Seidemann is cautious about Germany's future. "I would say positive. But we must keep watching. It's a fight. We can't sleep."

THE THEATRE is simple. Black walls, wooden folding chairs, and tables on which the audience can rest their tall glasses of beer. The stage set is simple too, just a long wooden bench placed as a prop for the actors in front of the piano. Burkhardt Seidemann explains some history of Jewish theatre to the crowd. Audience interaction begins immediately with a door prize awarded based on a ticket stub number. The winner is brought up on the stage and applauded.

Then in song, dance, and dialogue a man and woman, dressed as a poor Eastern European Jewish husband and wife, act out the pains and pleasures of their lives. At one point the two of them go out into the audience, she offering hunks of bread, he grabbing two young German women and pulling them up onto the stage. There he teaches them a few simple dance steps, and while he plays the spoons in time to the piano, he leaves them to dance together. When the music stops, they look disappointed that the dance is over. The scene ends and the two Germans return to their seats, laughing.

Despite the joy that these artists are sharing, the male lead, Mark Aizakowitch, says that as a Jew from the former Soviet Union he is often troubled by concerns of anti-Semitism. Still, he says, his life in Germany is otherwise satisfying. Satisfying, but not necessarily normal. He talks about being treated as "other" by Germans, likening it to being a beloved pet dog: petted, admired, cared for, but always reminded of his place. He sees that attitude not only toward Jews in Germany but all foreigners. "We are always somewhat limited. I feel I must know my place, no matter what I do, and not act better than others. So, watch out! There is a level over which you can't jump, no matter what you do. You stay always at the same level." Aizakowitch grew up in Ukraine speaking Yiddish. He's a bear of a man, with a head of hair approaching his collar and a full beard more salt than pepper. The easy joviality he shows on stage disappears as he talks about life in Germany. There is a sadness and some angst in his intense eyes.

I ask him if he feels he can live a normal life—like a German—in Berlin, as Jew and foreigner. "More or less, I believe," he says, "but not the same. We're the Jewish color, so to speak, in a large bunch of flowers." He's been in Germany for more than ten years, an assignment he's given himself because he too is convinced that the Germans need to learn about Jews. "There is no German culture without Jewish culture, without Jewish color. We bring, as do the Italians or the Americans or the Chinese, our color into this bouquet.

"We're living a full life here," says Aizakowitch, but he emphasizes that whenever he hears of an anti-Semitic attack, "like at the Potsdam cemetery, I'm afraid. Really I'm afraid. I'm not afraid for myself. I have a son, and he has also experienced anti-Semitism in school and in his basketball league. So I'm very careful." As is so common, he says, those who taunt his son know nothing about Jews or Jewish life. "The anti-Semitism problem is everywhere. I must say there is anti-Semitism even in America. But one must never forget that Germany has a special history with anti-Semitism. Therefore in Germany we're very . . . "—he searches for the correct word—"vulnerable."

His work at the theatre, says actor Mark Aizakowitch, offers hope, his arms outstretched as he speaks. "The theatre is like a fountain for us, where we can present our Jewish art. Here is a place where we integrate ourselves into German culture. Here the public comes. The audience is 99 percent German, not Jews. *Goyim sitzen*," he says with satisfaction, explaining that an audience of Gentiles fulfills his mission. "We're happy the Germans come here. They're our friends. I always say, one more person here in our theatre means one fewer person in the right wing. Jews must stay in Germany," Aizakowitch says. "We are missionaries here. We are bringing Jewish culture to the Germans, and that's very important."

Epilogue □ *Alexandr Rojsenblat Becomes a German Jew*

THE EXODUS TO BERLIN *is* a story of hope, renewal, and redemption. It is the story of a promise being kept by a new generation of Germans born with clean hands and taught a deep sense of responsibility for the sins of their grandparents. This is a generation of Germans that believes things can be made to change for the better when the lessons of history are known, taught, and lived with passion and persistence.

"The anti-Semite is in the unhappy position," Jean-Paul Sartre wrote, "of having a vital need for the very enemy he wishes to destroy." The resurgence of the Jewish population in Germany does provide the neo-Nazis fodder for their campaigns.

Popular slogans offer a glimpse into the feelings of a society. One of my favorite postcards from Germany reads, *"Ausländer, lasst uns mit den Deutschen nicht allein."* Foreigners, don't leave us alone with the Germans. The opposing point of view I spotted on a bumper sticker on a car that passed me on the Autobahn. The sticker mocked a slogan used by those Germans who are trying to defuse anti-foreigner prejudice. *"Wir sind alle Ausländer,"* is the original slogan, We are all foreigners. The amended version read, *"Wir sind alle Ausländer, fast überall,"* We are all foreigners, almost everywhere—a suggestion that foreigners are overrunning the country. At the entrance to the cathedral that dominates the skyline in Cologne, tourists are greeted by a poster picturing an intense-looking black woman in African tribal dress. There is a bank account number on the poster (for easy donation to the charity) and the message, "Love the foreigner as yourself."

TWO YEARS after exchanging his Ukraine papers for German citizenship, Alexandr Rojsenblat is enrolled at Potsdam University, studying economics and becoming a German. We last chatted while he was back in Ukraine for a brief visit, taking winter holidays with friends and family in Kiev. I called his Potsdam phone number and his German cell phone rang in Kiev.

"Have you missed Ukraine?" I ask him about his resettlement in Germany. His answer sums up the successful immigrant experience.

"Not very much," he says, "I miss Germany now!" He laughs. "I'm satisfied. It was the correct decision," he says about his move. "It was quite difficult, but now it's okay. I like Germany. The people in Germany are very nice. Germany is beautiful. You know, now I think that Ukraine is so dirty and dark. People are very angry here. My home now is Germany."

There were initial complications with Alexandr's application to Potsdam University: his papers from the university where he had been studying in Kiev were not in order. His parents, who spoke no German when they arrived in Potsdam, had problems finding good jobs. "It was difficult to fit in." But by the time we talked again, the three of them were settled in a pleasant apartment, his parents were working, and he was studying hard. "It's very difficult to study, but I'm doing my best. It's very hard to study economics in German," he tells me in his quite fluent English.

For the Rojsenblats there's been no prejudice expressed against them because they are from Ukraine, and no anti-Semitism. "I've seen some Nazis, some neo-Nazis, skinheads around the train station, but they have not bothered me. They didn't say anything."

I remind Alexandr that when we first met he told me he was going to be a German Jew. I ask him again, "Who are you?"

"I'm a Jew. I'm not a German Jew, though. I'm not German. I just live in Germany. I like Germany, but I cannot say I am German."

"Do you want to be German?" I ask.

"Yes, I think so. I like Germany. I want to be one of the German people. I want it to be 100 percent like home."

"Do you think that will happen?"

"I think yes. It takes time. Ten, fifteen years."

WHEN MY FAMILY AND I moved to Germany the year before the Wall was breached, things Jewish were hard to find. When an American friend of ours visited Berlin, we invited her to our flat in the Moabit neighborhood for lunch. Both her parents were Holocaust victims, concentration camp survivors. She was studying in Germany, trying to come to terms with her feelings about the country and its people. My wife decided to make her a familiar meal: a bagel with cream cheese and lox, piled high with tomatoes and onions. Trouble was, although some of the best breads in the world are baked in Germany, she could find no place in Berlin to buy bagels. That they weren't for sale, she says, probably fueled our appetites. "It suddenly seemed it would be terrific to have something from home." She found a bagel recipe in an old cookbook, *Laurel's Kitchen,** and spent hours in her own Berlin kitchen kneading the dough, letting it rise, punching it down, and repeating the procedure, then rolling out the dough, forming it into circles and boiling the bagels, next painting on the egg glaze, and finally baking them. It was, she remembers, "a long process. You can't just throw it

---

*My wife recommends ignoring Laurel's call for whole wheat flour and instead do as she did back in Berlin: substitute white flour for the whole wheat and enjoy a traditional-tasting bagel.

222

together, knead it a little, and stick it in the oven." But when our friend sat down to lunch, she cried. "Bagels in Berlin," she said over and over as she ate.

Today, finding a decent bagel in Berlin is no problem.

Notes

p. 26, on early evidence of Jews in Berlin, see Alexandra Richie, *Faust's Metropolis* (New York, 1998), p. 28.

p. 26, on restrictions against Jewish traders, see Anthony Read and David Fisher, *Berlin Rising: Biography of a City* (New York, 1994), p. 9.

p. 26, on taxing Jewish butchers, see Giles MacDonogh, *Berlin: A Portrait of Its History, Politics, Architecture, and Society* (New York, 1997, p. 21.

p. 27, "It would be hard to find . . . ," Will Durant, *The Reformation* (New York, 1957), p. 731.

p. 28, on *The Jews and Their Lies*, I found my copy distributed by a company called CPA Book Publisher. Operating via a post office box in Boring, Oregon, CPA also offers *International Jew: The World's Foremost Problem* by Henry Ford—an anthology, collected at Ford's direction, of excerpts from the *Protocols of the Elders of Zion*.

p. 28, "Admission of Fifty Families of Protected Jews," from Richie, *Faust's Metropolis*, p. 57.

p. 29, "a foreskin . . . ," Amos Elon, *The Pity of It All: A History of Jews in Germany, 1743–1933* (New York, 2002), p. 41.

p. 30, on the 1860 population of Jews in Berlin, see David Clay Large, *Berlin* (New York, 2000), p. 9.

p. 30, "No longer should false . . . ," Large, *Berlin*, p. 23.

p. 31, "The Jews are our misfortune . . . ," Richie, *Faust's Metropolis*, p. 251.

p. 31, on the Treitschkestrasse name-change controversy, see Reuben Bauddisch and Erik Kirschbaum, Reuters dispatch, November 18, 2002, "Ugly Berlin Dispute Raises Jewish Fears in Berlin."

p. 31, "I am a German . . . ," Otto Friedrich, *Before the Deluge: A Portrait of Berlin in the 1920s* (New York, 1972), p. 113.

p. 32, "All Jews were once . . . ," Joseph Roth, *The Wandering Jews* (New York, 2001), p. 21.

p. 32, "Our men will claim . . . ," Richie, *Faust's Metropolis*, p. 318.

p. 32, on Jewish soldiers' graves in the Weissensee cemetery, see MacDonogh, *Berlin: A Portrait of Its History, Politics, Architecture, and Society*, p. 20.

p. 32, "At every step . . . ," Friedrich, *Before the Deluge*, p. 82.

p. 33, on Rachkovsky being responsible for creating the *Protocols of the Elders of Zion*, see Walter Laqueur, *Black Hundred: The Rise of the Extreme Right in Russia* (New York, 1993), p. 35.

p. 33, "Without the clearest knowledge . . . ," Adolf Hitler, *Mein Kampf* (New York, 1971), p. 339.

p. 33, "Was there any form . . . ," Hitler, *Mein Kampf*, p. 57. Translator Ralph Mannheim chooses "kike" for Hitler's "Südlein."

p. 33, "With satanic joy . . . ," Hitler, *Mein Kampf*, p. 325.

p. 34, "I am a Jew . . . ," *Index on Censorship*, published by Writers & Scholars International, Ltd., London, issue 191, 1999, p. 57.

p. 34, "The nearly 150,000 Jews . . . ," Claudia Koonz, *Mothers in the Fatherland* (New York, 1987), p. 362.

p. 37, "Drive carefully . . . ," William L. Shirer, *The Rise and Fall of the Third Reich* (New York, 1959), p. 323. Shirer wrote that he was threatened with expulsion from Germany and was vilified on radio and in the print media for reporting that signs of this type were taken down during the 1936 Olympics when Berlin filled with foreign visitors.

p. 38, "By implication . . . ," Koonz, *Mothers in the Fatherland*, p. 372.

p. 38, "The government wants . . . ," "Germany Plans to Raise Status of Nation's Jews," *New York Times*, October 9, 2002.

p. 39, "The German Interior Ministry . . . ," Marc Fisher, *After the Wall* (New York, 1995), p. 213.

p. 39, "We want a free Europe . . . ," Yaron Svoray and Nick Taylor, *In Hitler's Shadow: An Israeli's Amazing Journey Inside Germany's Neo-Nazi Movement* (New York, 1994), p. 187.

p. 40, on defining a Jew, see "A Count of U.S. Jews Sees a Dip; Others Demur," *New York Times*, October 9, 2002.

p. 41, on Jews moving to Berlin to escape early Nazi attacks elsewhere in Germany, see Leonard Gross, *The Last Jews in Berlin* (New York, 1982), p. 13.

p. 41, on Jews living underground in Berlin during the war, see Koonz, *Mothers in the Fatherland*, p. 378.

p. 42, on the number of Jews who survived the war in Berlin, see Hans Rothfels, *The German Opposition to Hitler* (Chicago, 1962), p. 33.

p. 51, on Jews in Displaced Persons camps in postwar Germany, see Tad Szulc, *The Secret Alliance: The Extraordinary Story of the Rescue of the Jews Since World War II* (New York, 1991), p. 169.

p. 54, on Spiegel's fear of immigrants posing as Jews, see "Jewish Leader Urges Immigration Reform," a BBC report by Patrick Barlett, June 24, 2001.

p. 55, "The new era dawned . . . ," Wladimir Kaminer, *Russian Disco: Tales of Everyday Lunacy on the Streets of Berlin* (London, 2002), p. 14.

p. 57, the Douglas Rushkoff op-ed ran in the November 20, 2002, *New York Times*.

p. 57, "There are three ways . . . ," Peter Gay, *My German Question: Growing Up in Nazi Berlin* (New Haven, 1998), p. 111.

p. 62, "As the guy walked . . . ," "Unsettling Return to Germany," *Los Angeles Times*, October 22, 2002.

p. 76, "Whenever Israel is discussed . . . ," "The Longest Journey: A Survey of Migration," *Economist*, May 25, 2002.

p. 76, "If I have injured . . . ," "Small Party Tries to Calm Uproar Over Slurs About Jews," *New York Times*, June 7, 2002. On Möllemann resigning as the FPD vice chairman, see the *International Herald Tribune*, September 24, 2002.

p. 77, "West Germany is . . . ," Alan Tigay, *The Jewish Traveler* (Northvale, N.J., 1994), p. 54.

p. 77, "I, for example . . . ," "Weizman Cannot Understand How Jews Live in Germany," Reuters Information Service, January 14, 1996.

p. 77, "The majority of applicants . . . ," "Israelis Turn to Berlin for Refuge from Conflict," London *Guardian*, June 17, 2002.

p. 81, on the *Judenkarte*, see Peter Wyden, *Wall: The Inside Story of Divided Berlin* (New York, 1989), p. 655.

p. 81, "The first freely chosen . . . ," Robert Darnton, *Berlin Journal: 1989–1990* (New York, 1991), p. 283.

p. 90, "There are Eastern Jewish criminals . . . ," Roth, *Wandering Jews*, p. 69.

p. 98, on Estrongo Nachama, see Jonathan Kaufman, *A Hole in the Heart of the World: Being Jewish in Eastern Europe* (New York, 1997), p. 65.

p. 105, on the November 1992 demonstration, see Fisher, *After the Wall*, p. 276.

p. 106, "To merely tolerate . . . ," Elon, *The Pity of It All*, p. 45.

p. 109, Andrew Roth's guidebook is *The Goldapple Guide to Jewish Berlin*, published by Goldapple Publishers, Berlin.

p. 120, on Pastor Niemöller's resistance to Hitler, see Large, *Berlin*, p. 307, and Shirer, *Rise and Fall of the Third Reich*, p. 325.

p. 121, "First they came . . . ," Richie, *Faust's Metropolis*, p. 540.

p. 123, "Jewish foreigners . . . ," Fisher, *After the Wall*, p. 207.

p. 129, "Forbidding a party . . . ," "Germany Seeks Ban on Neo-Nazis," Associated Press dispatch, November 8, 2000.

p. 129, "I defended Mahler . . . ," "The Left Arm of the Law," Deutsche Welle television documentary, Cologne, 2002.

p. 148, "A firebomb badly . . . ," "Holocaust Museum Burned in Germany," *New York Times*, September 6, 2002.

p. 172, "The NPD is using its money . . . ," the German government publishes an annual report on right-wing extremism and posts it on the Foreign Ministry's website.

p. 177, on *Rücksack Berliners*, see Read and Fisher, *Berlin Rising*, p. 2.

p. 182, "The NPD is on tour . . . ," "State's Worsening Economy Gives Boost to Right-Wing Extremism," *Frankfurter Allgemeine Zeitung*, January 18, 2001.

p. 184, "Germany is trying . . . ," "Neo-Nazis Sheltering Web Sites in the United States," *Washington Post*, December 21, 2000.

p. 184, "You know what . . . ," "German Neo-Nazis Post List of Targets on the Internet," London *Guardian*, November 3, 1999.

p. 184, "Here you can publish . . . ," "State's Worsening Economy Gives Boost to Right-Wing Extremism," *Frankfurter Allgemeine Zeitung*, January 18, 2001.

p. 185, "In order to have . . . ," "Neo-Nazis Sheltering Web Sites in the United States," Peter Finn, *Washington Post*, December 21, 2000.

p. 200, "Ninety percent of pupils . . . ," "State's Worsening Economy Gives Boost to Right-Wing Extremism," *Frankfurter Allegemeine Zeitung*, January 18, 2001.

p. 201, on the report of David B.'s arrest, see "Neo-Nazi Youths Arrested in Germany," Associated Press dispatch, December 27, 2000.

p. 203, "It's been like this . . . ," "Germany's Rampant Racism," *San Francisco Chronicle*, October 2, 2000.

p. 207, "There's no chance . . . ," "As Eastern Germany Rusts, Young Workers Leave," *New York Times*, December 25, 2002.

p. 220, "The anti-Semite is in the unhappy position . . . ," Norman G. Finkelstein, *The Holocaust Industry: Reflections on the Exploitation of Jewish Suffering* (New York, 2001), p. 34.

Index

A NOTE ON THE AUTHOR

Peter Laufer was born in New York City and studied at the University of California, Berkeley, and at American University in Washington, D.C. He worked in radio in San Francisco and Los Angeles before becoming a correspondent for NBC News. Working out of Washington, he covered breaking news worldwide and created documentaries, many of them award-winning. He won the George Polk Award for his documentary on Americans imprisoned overseas, and Edward R. Murrow and National Headliner awards for his documentary work on immigration, drug trafficking, and illiteracy. His film on the subject of *Exodus to Berlin*, produced with Jeff Kamen, was awarded the David Wolper Documentary Film Prize. Mr. Laufer is at present an independent journalist and writer; he has also written *Iron Curtain Rising* and *Nightmare Abroad*, among other books. He is married with two sons and lives in Sonoma County, California.